the balanced *breakthrough*

the balanced breakthrough

Winning at Work Without Losing at Life

Garrett Maroon

THE BALANCED BREAKTHROUGH: Winning at Work Without Losing at Life
© 2025 by Garrett Maroon

All rights reserved. No part of this publication may be reproduced, stored in a retrieval system, or transmitted in any form by any means, electronic, mechanical, photocopy, recording, or otherwise, without the prior permission of the publisher, except as provided by USA copyright law.

No patent liability is assumed with respect to the use of the information contained herein. Although every precaution has been taken in the preparation of this book, the publisher and author assume no responsibility for errors or omissions. Neither is any liability assumed for damages resulting from the use of the information contained herein.

Published by Forefront Books, Nashville, Tennessee.
Distributed by Simon & Schuster.

Scripture quotations marked esv are taken from The ESV® Bible (The Holy Bible, English Standard Version®), © 2001 by Crossway, a publishing ministry of Good News Publishers.

Scripture quotations marked niv are taken from the Holy Bible, New International Version®, NIV®. Copyright © 1973, 1978, 1984, 2011 by Biblica, Inc.™ Used by permission of Zondervan. All rights reserved worldwide. www.zondervan.com The "NIV" and "New International Version" are trademarks registered in the United States Patent and Trademark Office by Biblica, Inc.™

Excerpts from "The Dash" poem, written by Linda Ellis, © Southwestern Family of Companies, Used by Permission.

Library of Congress Control Number: 2025916057

Print ISBN: 978-1-63763-475-2
E-book ISBN: 978-1-63763-476-9

Cover Design by George Stevens
Interior Design by PerfecType, Nashville, TN

Printed in the United States of America
25 26 27 28 29 30 LAK 10 9 8 7 6 5 4 3 2

DEDICATION

This book is dedicated to my beautiful and amazing wife, Rachel, and our five wild, rambunctious, and loving kids—Haddie, Dylan, Ivy, Zoe, and Miles. You are the reason I work hard to succeed professionally and stay fully present at home. You're the reason I want to win. I love you all.

table of contents

Part 1: The Story

Chapter 1: The Dash — 13
Chapter 2: My Story — 21
Chapter 3: The Typical Agent Story — 33

Part 2: The Scoreboard

Chapter 4: The Industry Is Wrong — 49
Chapter 5: Reclaiming an Intentional Life — 63
Chapter 6: Creating the Scoreboard — 77

Part 3: The PDA Formula

Chapter 7: Authenticity — 95
Chapter 8: Predictability — 129
Chapter 9: Profitability — 157
Chapter 10: My Personal PDA Formula — 185

TABLE OF CONTENTS

Part 4: Intentional Achievement

Chapter 11: Hierarchy of Attention   201
Chapter 12: Rule of 8s   213
Chapter 13: The Right Next Thing   219

Chapter 14: Conclusion: So What?   229

Acknowledgments   233
Endnotes   237

part 1
The Story

I am a real estate agent by trade. I have been since 2014. I've gone through the variations the industry offers—from being an agent on a team to having my own team to getting out of production (no longer actively selling and letting my team handle the day-to-day) with just one agent and one admin. I've also even ventured into other businesses—coaching, training, Amazon selling, speaking, investing, and now writing this book. Some have gone well and some haven't.

I've learned that business principles stay the same throughout different industries; just the tactics change. In real estate, I may generate business by sitting down with a past client for coffee, but if I were a car salesman with long hours at the dealership, I might focus on calling those clients. If I am trying to sell my coaching services, it is more of a direct call to action, much like the approach of most salespeople across the industry. Selling online is much more about traffic, views, keywords, and so on, and much less about personal relationships.

I write this book with a background in many versions of "being a salesperson," and though these pages will draw heavily on my experience as a real estate professional and is written with them in mind, other professionals can certainly find value here. I welcome you to read on and apply the principles you discover here to your life and industry, whatever that may be.

The book is designed to be practical and theoretical. My aim is that you will think differently and act differently by the end.

Real estate is my vocation, but most importantly, I'm a Christian, a husband, and a father of five. I will occasionally quote the Bible to illustrate a point, but this book is written to anyone of any faith background. Being a husband and a dad of so many littles (the oldest is only eight as of this writing) has made this content even more important and applicable in my life. *How do I win at work without losing at life?* became my most-used mantra to reset and refocus my time, energy, and attention.

Wrestling with that question is what led to my breakthrough and what I believe can lead to yours. So, no matter where you are in life—young, old, married, single, parent, non-parent, Christian, not Christian—we all share a common thread. We all want to win at work without losing at life. The chapters that follow will help you do exactly that.

I want you to become more profitable, in a more consistent way, all while being as authentic as possible and showing up well for the people in your life. I want you to win.

Are you ready for that? Then read on!

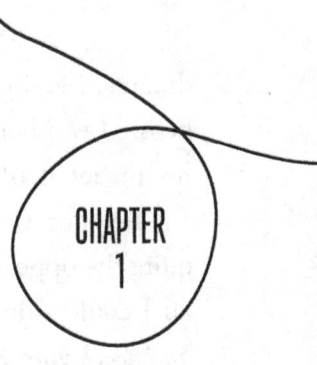

CHAPTER 1

The Dash

Not too long ago, I was standing in Christiansburg, Virginia, at the graveside of my grandmother. She was an incredible woman who had finally succumbed to Parkinson's after a long and arduous journey. She was being buried next to "Papa," my grandfather, a World War II veteran and successful businessman. Buried next to him was *his* father, my great-grandfather, Harvey Ridinger. As I read his faded name and the dates—1885 *dash* 1957—I remember thinking, *This is my great-grandfather, but all I know about him is what's on his headstone: the year he was born and the year he died.*

I had no emotions associated with his passing. I did not know if he had fought in World War I, if he had been successful in a vocation, or if he had struggled his whole life. I didn't know his thoughts, his hopes, his dreams, his life. He had died only thirty-seven years before I was born, and yet I did not know him and felt no impact at all looking at his headstone.

I do not write this to be morbid or to cast us down; quite the opposite. As I looked again at his headstone, all I could think was, *That dash between his birth year and death year was his whole life.*

As I looked again at his headstone, all I could think was, That dash between his birth year and death year was his whole life.

Whether it was lived well, poorly, or somewhere in between, that dash was his life. Did he spend it on fading pursuits like more money, more fame, and more recognition, or did he spend it on lasting pursuits like loving his wife, shaping his son, and giving more than he took? I don't know. In fact, it's possible *no one* knows anymore. No matter how hard he may have strived after things in his life, he's now just a name, some dates, and a dash.

One day, that's all that'll be left of me too.

The same goes for you, for all of us.

So, the question is, What did he do with his dash? And more importantly, what will each of us do with ours? Will we spend it in vain pursuit of personal glory, more money, more success, bigger businesses, nicer cars, higher sales rankings, more stuff? Or will we choose to spend it on what we truly hold important?

I want to start off this book by putting our lives and businesses into perspective. This excerpt from Linda Ellis's poem "The Dash" does an excellent job framing it for us:

> I read of a man who stood to speak
> at the funeral of a friend.
> He referred to the dates on the tombstone
> from the beginning to the end.
>
> He noted first came the date of birth
> and spoke the following date with tears.
> But he said what mattered most of all
> was the dash between the years.
>
> For that dash represents all the time
> that they spent alive on Earth.
> And now only those who loved them
> know what that little line is worth.
>
> For it matters not how much we own
> the cars, the house, the cash.
> What matters is how we live and love,
> and how we spend our dash.

So, think about this long and hard.
Are there things you'd like to change?
For you never know how much time is left
that can still be rearranged.

. . .

So, when your eulogy is being read
with your life's actions to rehash,
would you be proud of the things they say
about how you spent your dash?[1]

As one of my favorite pastors, Voddie Baucham, always says, "If you can't say *amen*, say *ouch*."

That poem hits deep every time I read it. Maybe it hits you hard too. I suspect it does. The truth is, most of us have become something other than what we intended to be. We've allowed the stress and chaos of our industries, whether it's real estate or something else, to disrupt the intentionality of our lives. We've too often traded dinner with our kids for the "urgent" client call or can't-wait project. We've too often spent our "vacations" sitting on the beach, laptop in hand, writing an offer or catching up on emails. Worst of all, *we've worn this as a badge of honor.* We've too often damaged or sadly even lost relationships, all for the sake of "success."

If that's you, it's okay. We've all been there in one way or another. But here's the good news: There is hope. Hope to reclaim an intentional life, all while closing more deals—in less time and doing it more authentically. That's why I wrote this book. Because I care about your life. I care about your relationships. I care about your health. I care about your finances. I care about your business. And I know there's a better way.

The truth is, most of us have become something other than what we intended to be.

Here's a sneak peek into where we are going. The book is broken into four different parts, each building on one another. I encourage you to read from start to finish and not skip around. And yes, I do mean reading *to finish* (I'm looking at you, habitual halfway reader who has six books on your desk or nightstand that you've started and never completed). You'll see that this is a pretty short book. That's not because I couldn't think of more to say; I kept it short on purpose to honor your time and encourage you to read all the way through. Oh, and one more thing, you'll notice I can be pretty straightforward. I don't believe in sugarcoating the problems. If you go to the doctor for a diagnosis, you need them to tell you straight. That's my intent too. We won't waste time—we will go straight to the heart of the problem.

In part 1 of the book, we will explore *The Story*. Here, I will share my own journey that brought me to the point of writing this book. I'll also reveal how I personally fell prey to the real estate industry's definition of success and the wake-up call that caused me to write my own scoreboard and define success on my own terms. Then, we will get really honest about the typical agent's path and the challenges brought on by the industry trying to create a one-size-fits-all approach.

In part 2, we will dive deep into *creating* the balanced breakthrough by building your own *Scoreboard*, beginning with why the real estate industry is wrong and has been leading agents in a dangerous direction for decades. Then, we will reset our minds and our hearts around what is truly important to us. And finally we'll work together to build your first-ever personal scoreboard to launch your new life of intentionality and purpose.

In part 3, I will lay out my *PDA Formula*. And no, I'm not talking about the PDA that got you in trouble in the high school lunchroom or behind the bleachers between classes—public displays of affection. No, my version of PDA is a formula I personally use and teach to help real estate agents and other professionals create a **P**redictable, **D**ollar-Productive (Profitable) business that **A**ligns with who you are. Using the PDA Formula will equip you to achieve your new intentional life and start winning at work without losing at life.

Finally, in part 4, we will finish with *Intentional Achievement* and examine how controlling your attention will change your life. I want to leave you with some very simple yet extremely helpful tools to stay on track. Consider these as guardrails for your scoreboard to keep you from straying too far from where you want to go. I'll share how to create a hierarchy of attention, how to utilize the Rule of 8s in your lead generation, and how to determine your right next thing.

This book will be succinct and to the point. Remember, I actually want you to finish it, and—as a husband, a father of five, and an active real estate agent myself—I know how busy your life is and the demands on your time.

Here's my vision for you, for me, for our entire industry:

- That agents everywhere would have better businesses, ones that free us up to more time in our day—time to spend more intentionally in the lasting pursuits of life.
- That the kids of agents everywhere would grow up with a mom or dad who knows when and how to put their phone away and give them their full attention.

- That families would be restored that have been pulled apart by the urgency of the market.
- That agents would no longer be defined or define themselves only by their real estate stat sheet (number of homes sold, volume, and Gross Commission Income) but by the true joys of life—being a good spouse, a good parent, and a good friend.
- That we would *win at work without losing at life*.

Are you in? Let's get this story started.

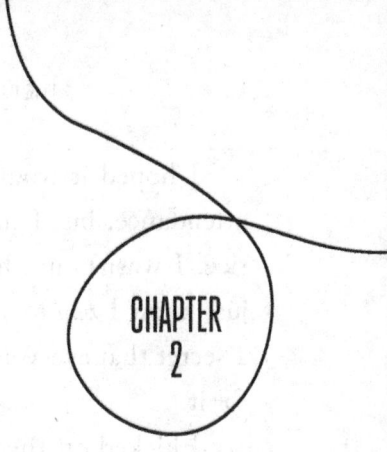

CHAPTER 2

My Story

It was about two hours after I had shared a message very similar to the one you are going to read about in this book. I was speaking at a one-day conference just outside of Richmond, Virginia, at a sprawling, gothic-styled castle in the country.

More than a hundred real estate agents had shown up to grow their businesses and take their mindsets to a new level. There were a lot of wonderful speakers lined up, and the room was full of top producers. The talk I was planning to give (that then became this book) was brand-new and untested, and I had written it at the last minute. It wasn't that I had been lazy or had been procrastinating—though those are two skills I most certainly and regrettably have; it was relatively new information and insight that had been stirring quietly within me. And now, it was demanding to be set free.

I hoped it would make an impact on *someone* in attendance, but I hadn't even had a chance to practice. I wasn't sure how long (or how short) it was; I just knew I *had* to share it. It felt like I had unlocked a secret that everyone needed to know. So, I just went for it.

I kicked off the day with my new talk titled "The Common Agent Scoreboard." Another speaker came up after me and spoke on social media. Both talks seemed to be well received, but I still wasn't sure my emerging concept—this new "secret" I shared—had landed the way I hoped it would.

We were taking our first break of the day when a woman in her forties walked up to me and introduced herself as a solo agent and a mom. "Garrett," she said, "I really appreciated your talk. I sold fifty-five homes last year, which was my best year ever. Now, everyone has been asking me what I am going to do this year, and I've been telling them I will sell sixty or seventy homes because that's what we're supposed to do in this industry, right? We sell more and more and more as if nothing is ever good enough. But after hearing your talk, I've decided I'm not going to aim for sixty or seventy sales; I'm going to intentionally sell *thirty* homes this year, and it's going to change my life!"

Now, you may wonder what kind of real estate talk encourages someone to sell *fewer* homes. Don't worry,

MY STORY

I promise that's not the point of this book. So how could selling fewer homes change this one agent's life?

The truth is, this successful woman wasn't the first person whose life was changed by the concepts we will explore together in this book. These principles had already changed my life . . . and I believe they can change yours too. And if you make it all the way to the last page, you'll hear how it changed her life too.

We sell more and more and more as if nothing is ever good enough.

For me, it all started in 2021. I had been married for almost ten years, I had three kids at the time (ages four, two, and newborn), I'd been in real estate since 2014, and I had been a top-producing agent for many years. I was doing what top agents are "supposed" to do: I had a team of three agents and three admins working with me. We had just sold one hundred homes that year, all by referral. The team was happy. I was happy. Everyone was making money. Life was pretty good at the Maroon Group, my team in Hampton Roads, Virginia (which is now called the 2:10 Realty Group).

All was well. Until it wasn't.

One day, I came to a crossroads in my business. It was time for something different. Truth be told, everything was working *so* well that I had gotten bored—bored of the monotony of success. So, it was time for a change. You probably already know that the entrepreneur's brain can be both a wonderful and a very dangerous place. We seek the thrill of the chase and will sometimes even blow things up that are working just to give us something to fix. That can be fun, but it's not always good. This was me.

It was a beautiful, Virginia summer afternoon—75 degrees and sunny, birds chirping, lawnmowers mowing, people peopling—and I was on my back deck doing some thinking. "Thinking time" sessions, which I'd discovered in *The Road Less Stupid* by Keith Cunningham, had become a rhythm in my week.[2] It was time I dedicated to breaking away from "doing work" and focusing on the vision—working *on* the business instead of just *in* the business, as they say. My wife, Rachel, and our kiddos were gone that day, and the house and yard were quiet. So, I took advantage of it.

My pen never stopped moving as new answers, new ideas, and new possibilities filled my mind. It's amazing what the brain is capable of if we just give it some space to work. Before I knew it, I had a plan. It was a good plan. In fact, I honestly think it was a *great* plan. It was a plan to double my profits in the next twelve months. But there was one small problem: I couldn't figure out how to double my profits without also increasing the amount of time I spent at work.

You see, I had worked my butt off for a few years to build my referral business since I didn't grow up in this area, and by this point, I was enjoying the fruits of my labor. I had sold fifty homes beginning in my second year in the industry and every year since then. But now, with a team, I barely had to spend forty hours a week working myself for us to sell a hundred homes. It was a huge blessing.

So, I was faced with a dilemma: Work more hours and earn more money . . . or stay right where I was financially and try to figure out how to work even less. As the afternoon sun warmed the deck, I sketched out a way to double my profits, but doing so would ramp me back up to about fifty or sixty hours a week. Or, I could stay at my current profit level . . . and probably *cut* my hours down to fifteen or twenty a week.

In a moment of clarity, a question came to mind: *Five years from now, if I could look back on the person sitting here right now, today, in this very moment, who would I be most proud of—the guy who chose the sixty-hour work week for the bigger paycheck or the guy who chose the current paycheck, intentionally reduced his hours, and spent more time with his wife and kids?*

The answer was obvious when I posed it that way. I'd be most proud of the guy who chose his wife and young kids over making more money—money that, frankly, we didn't truly *need*. Money that would have done more for my *ego account* than my *bank account*. I was really thankful for the clarity of that question.

But as I pondered the answer to that question, it started to bring up even more questions. *If that was what I really wanted—more time with my wife and kids—then why was I even doing what I was already doing? Why did I build a bigger team? Did I even want a big team? Did I even want to spend all my working hours selling real estate, or did I desire to do other things?*

Again, my team members were awesome, our business was doing well, and we were still one hundred percent referral; yet I didn't like the size and complexity of the operation. I love simple, easy, compact. That's literally how I'm built—five foot seven (okay, five foot six and three-quarters) and stocky (thank you, donuts). I like compact. Suddenly it hit me like a pie in the face after losing a summer-cookout contest: *I didn't want what I had built.* (And yes, I will use as many culinary references as possible because food is amazing—and not just donuts and pie.)

Have you ever had that moment when you stop and wonder why you're even doing what you're doing? Well, this was my moment.

As I was asking myself those questions, it hit me. The light bulb moment. No, I didn't want a big team; I had *never* wanted a big team. No, I didn't want to spend all my working hours selling real estate.

What *did* I want?

I wanted a small team. I wanted to be out of production. I wanted to take what I had learned and share it with other agents. I wanted the freedom to take Fridays off and go to the pool with Rachel and the kids. I wanted to enjoy these precious few years I had with them while they were young. And I didn't want it to take me another decade before I could do that just because I was chasing after "a better life for my family." We were blessed to be in a position where we didn't *need* more money to support our current lifestyle. You know what my family *did* need for "a better life"? Me. At home. Laughing and playing. Available for walks around the block, weekend getaways, and spur-of-the-moment pool days. My kids wanted to see Daddy right now, not fifteen years from now when they'd practically be moving out of the house.

You see, I had been chasing what Gary Keller calls the "7th level team" in his book *The Millionaire Real Estate Agent*.[3] That's a large and complex real estate team run by a CEO that allows the owner to step out of the business and continue to be highly profitable. I thought that was the only way out of selling real estate 24/7. Truthfully, though, I'd never even met anyone who had gotten to that point, and yet I was chasing what felt unattainable. I didn't think there was another option, so I just kept doing what I'd been doing, striving toward all I knew to strive for—what the industry told me was the pinnacle of success.

As I dug into it, I wanted to really understand *why* I had even built the team in the first place. All it did was require more time and energy from me—energy I neither had nor wanted to give. So why was I acting so counter to what I truly wanted? It didn't make sense.

I came in from the backyard and walked back up to my office, still kicking questions around my brain, and it was then that everything became clear. There on my whiteboard in the middle of my office were written three items:

1. Number of transactions
2. Total sales volume
3. Net profit

That was it. Those were the only three numbers I was tracking. I was just measuring what the industry told me to measure; what else would I do? I was doing what I had been taught, like the kid in class who sits in the front row, takes notes, and does exactly what the teacher says. There was nothing else on that whole board but transactions, volume, profit.

MY STORY

I'm the guy who's always said my family is what's most important to me. That's why I got into real estate.

I'm the guy who always said I cared more about time with them than I did about the money in the bank, but where were they on my whiteboard's metrics of "success"? The only things I was tracking to determine whether I was succeeding or not were deals and money. I was measuring only what *the industry* had told me was important; I wasn't measuring what *I* said was important.

So, of course, every decision I made was to improve my measurements. I had to add more agents to the team to sell more homes and make more money. I had to work more hours to generate more leads, increase my volume, and make more money. I had nothing else to base decisions on, no other way to keep score.

But what if that's not why I got into the industry in the first place? What if instead of selling a crazy number of homes, making a stupid amount of money, and being the top agent in the office, I wanted to show up well for my family? What if I wanted to create my own scoreboard and measure what *I* thought was important, not what the industry told me to care about?

In that moment, everything changed.

From that day on, I changed the game. I was no longer willing to play the industry's game of success. I was playing by my own rules. I had reclaimed my own life by creating my own scoreboard—and I want you to do the same. To have the same breakthrough I've had.

I was no longer willing to play the industry's game of success. I was playing by my own rules.

Success should not be defined by your coworker out there hustling and selling more homes than you while you stay home with your kids and sell "only" five homes a year. Success should not be defined by an industry or a broker that makes money only when we, the agents, trade time with the important people in our lives just to increase our sales numbers. Your success should be defined by one and only one person: *you*. Comparison is a foul mistress. Stop looking at everyone else just to figure out whether you're winning the game. Start looking at what you know is important and define what success looks like to you.

Life is much more than just selling homes, and you are much more than just a real estate agent.

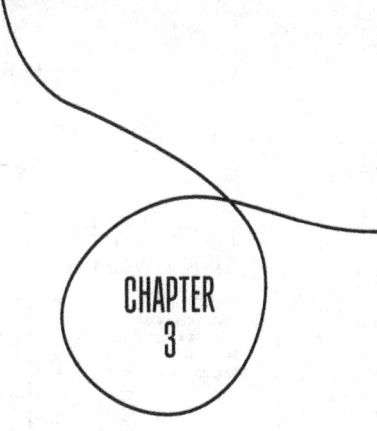

CHAPTER 3

The Typical Agent Story

We were on the way to church. My wife was in the passenger seat, my two littlest (ages two and ten months) in the middle seats, and my two oldest (six and four) in the back seat.

Dylan, my four-year-old son: "Daddy, guess what?"

Me: "What, buddy?"

Dylan: "Did you know you could build an awesome dinosaur with Legos?"

Me: "No, I didn't, buddy. That's really cool. Do you want to build it after church?"

Dylan: "No, I can't build it. I don't have enough patience."

The wisdom (or was it a lack of determination?) of my four-year-old son is not unlike the typical real estate agent's path.

Typical Agent Path

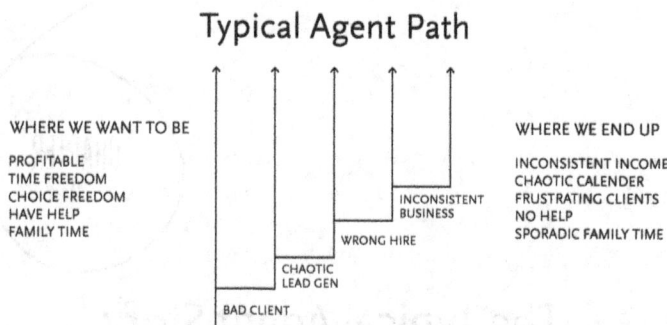

Everyone has good intentions when they start. No one would launch a new business with the goal of low profits, crazy schedules, and a frustrating business. We start with such optimism on sticking to the path and then . . . *people*. This job would be so easy if people weren't involved.

Everyone has good intentions when they start. No one would launch a new business with the goal of low profits, crazy schedules, and a frustrating business.

Here's how it happens: We have a beautiful, romanticized goal of the perfect business. Day one, we head in that direction in a blissful cloud of pure delight. But then, *dun dun dun!* . . . a bad client enters the picture. This client takes up way too much time, causes way too much headache, and interrupts way too many dinners. Bad client—1. Your blissful business—0. You've just been knocked off course.

You try to right yourself and recover from the bad client, and just as you start to get yourself upright again, you take a class on social media. You hear about other agents' successes online, and you beat yourself up a little since you aren't doing social like they are. So, you decide you need to incorporate social media strategies on top of your already chaotic lead generation plan. You've just been knocked back off course.

But you're tough, you're committed, and you're a hard worker, so despite being a little wayward, you pull yourself together and get to work.

Your business starts to grow, and it's time to hire an employee. Problem is, you're so busy that there is no time to learn *how* to hire. You need help *right now* to ease your busyness pain, so you make a quick (or should I say *desperate*) hire without the proper vetting, training, or understanding. And—big surprise—the person you hired turns out to be a bad fit. Now, you're even *more* off track.

Then, the worry from the inconsistent business and its up-and-down income starts to keep you up at night. Sleeplessness, anxiety, and a few extra pounds from late-night stress eating cause your blood pressure to skyrocket. You grasp at anything and everything to get your pipeline back to where it was, but all you get is an expensive, false promise from companies that sell you what they claim to be qualified leads but end up being worthless. Now, you're *even further* off track, and your wallet is much lighter from all the money you've wasted on bad hires and crummy leads.

Discouragement sets in. You're so far from the perfect business you envisioned that you need binoculars to even see the path you intended to follow. It almost feels like every day takes you one (or ten) steps backward, moving you further and further from your goals no matter how hard and how long you work.

Does any of this sound familiar?

This tragic story is all too common in our industry. What was meant to *give* you the life you desired has now become the very thing that *stands in the way* of that life. The promise of "a life by design" quickly becomes an unattainable concept.

The longer I've been in business, the more I've realized the biggest challenge we face every day is not "What do I do?" or even "How do I do it?" The biggest challenge, as I see it, is simply showing up with a belief that we *can do it*.

I can no longer count on my two hands (and two feet) the number of times I've wondered if I was any good at this whole real estate thing and whether I should even stay in the industry. I can no longer count the number of times I've convinced myself I would fail and should just quit. I've bought into what everyone around me said as if my unique strengths did not matter and there was only one path to success.

At the start of my career, it took me five and a half months to sell my first home. Even that was a miracle because Rachel and I had agreed at the three-month mark that I would quit the industry. Thankfully, we hung on three more months, and I made my first deal with just days to spare.

I was laughed at by my own brokerage team leader when, two years in, I said I wanted to sell fifty homes a year while working less than forty hours a week, all by referral. The leader whose job it was to encourage me and help me grow laughed at me and said it wasn't possible.

I've gone to all the classes and learned all the sales strategies and techniques. I learned exactly what all the top performers were doing. I can't tell you how many times I wondered if I needed to give up my dream of becoming successful on my terms and just accept a life chasing the hamster wheel of sales while missing out too often on the joys of life. Here's a secret they don't want you to know: The industry owns the wheel, and we are the hamster they don't want to let off.

Maybe you've felt that way a time or two as well.

Most of us get into real estate to create a better life for ourselves and our families. Maybe we saw how much our agent was paid when we bought a home and thought, *I can do that too.* Or we realized our W-2 job was not progressing quickly enough, and we refused to wait around for a 5 percent raise (that was my experience). Maybe you were tired of your boss telling you when and where you had to work. Tired of asking permission to take off the day before Thanksgiving to be with your family. Tired of having your life dictated by someone else who was focused on their own bottom line.

Most of us want to make more money and have more freedom. We view the "good life" as $100,000 a year with total autonomy in how we spend our days. These are excellent goals.

Then, we run smack-dab into the problem. The life we desire, the life we thought we were getting, is actually being blocked by the very thing we thought would bring it—our business. We thought the freeing life we wanted was as easy as moving our ladders from the W-2 wall to the business-owner wall. In reality, we moved our ladders and only later realized how high that business-owner wall was and how long it would take to climb to the life we wanted at the top.

So, most of us become discouraged, disheartened, and disenfranchised. We set out with such high hopes, but after taking hit after hit to our beliefs, we eventually give up and accept that we will never have the life we wanted. Sadly, it has been said that 87 percent of agents even quit the business within five years. After riding that emotional roller coaster of extreme excitement to extreme defeat, we accept that the life we desire and see other people have is just a dream that we can never bring into reality—or at least *our* reality.

That's when we start to settle. We settle for mediocrity. We settle for a life of weekend open houses, five minutes to answer the "lead," always working on vacation, and being open 24/7. All those cracks in the foundation of our life start to widen and expand, creeping into one area after another until it feels like our whole being is teetering on the edge of a bottomless pit.

We might think we're putting on a good show, but the people around us—including our clients—can see it. Just as they noticed in the house we just showed them, our buyers (and sellers) can tell those cracks have been there a long time and aren't going away anytime soon.

We assumed we could do business our own way. After all, we still love people and love houses; isn't that enough? But our runways were too short. We didn't give ourselves enough time to get the plane off the ground, so we abandoned our whole vision for our life with real estate and accepted a less-than-ideal life . . . or thought about quitting.

I refuse to accept that all these enormous failures in our industry should just be written off as "normal." I want to flip the script from 87 percent failure rate to 87 percent success rate. You *can* do it.

You aren't failing the industry. The industry is failing you.

Read that again. I believe the two keys to long-term success and excitement—not to mention finding that life you always wanted—are *authenticity* and a *personal scoreboard*. The industry has told you to run in the wrong direction for so long that you've lost that dream in your heart. No more! That exhausting race toward burnout ends here and now. It's time to reclaim the dream you started with—and not just reclaim it but bring it to life. It's time to stop being the fake-smile, glossy-head-shot version of yourself that you plaster on For Sale signs, billboards, and social media. It's time to stop trying to follow the same formulas and tactics that might work for other agents who are happy to log eighty hours a week and eat fast-food dinners in their cars every night. It's time to realign with who you really are, fully embrace what you want for your life (even if it's less than what you've been told you *should* want), and become the very best version of your unique self you can possibly be. It's time for a *breakthrough*.

THE TYPICAL AGENT STORY

As I write this, I have just finished my tenth year in real estate. I've sold more than six hundred and fifty homes and $250 million in volume, and I've done it all exactly how God wired me to work—by relationship.

It's time to reclaim the dream you started with—and not just reclaim it but bring it to life.

As I mentioned, I didn't grow up where I now work and live. I started with only forty people in my sales database, and today, I have only two hundred and eighty-seven in that database. I started as an agent on someone else's team in 2014 before launching my own in 2016. Just five years later, in 2021, I stepped out of production (my team was now running all day-to-day operations without me) with only one agent and one admin. In 2022, the three of us sold eighty-six homes, all by relationship, for a gross commission income of $900,000. I spent only $10,000 total for the year on lead generation. We had a 9,000 percent ROI, and I worked only five hours a week in the business. My scoreboard was achieved. My life was full.

And if I can do it, I know you can.

Your dream business is possible.

The PDA Formula works.

Here's a peek into the life it's allowed me to have: I'm married to my best friend, Rachel, and together we have five kiddos. Haddie is eight, Dylan is six, Ivy Lane is four, Zoe is two, and Miles is two months. I start work at 9:00 a.m., and I finish at 5:00 p.m., so I'm home with them every night. I take every seventh week off to be with the family and every other Friday morning off to go on a day date with my wife, and I rarely work a weekend.

We host Bible study every Thursday and are actively involved in our church. I cofounded the 2:10 Collective on the eXp Realty platform to get into business with Christian agents all over the world. I host a weekly podcast called *The Faithful Agent*, started a nonprofit called The Faithful Agent, coach agents, teach and train weekly, wrote this book, and even try to be cool on Instagram—and I do it all in under forty hours a week. I made a commitment that I would not miss my kids' childhood years, so I'm making it work by measuring success my own way and using the PDA Formula to turn my authenticity into a profitable business.

Why do I share all of this with you? It's certainly not to brag; I've made plenty of mistakes. One of my businesses has been around for three years and is totally, absolutely crushing it—raking in a grand total of (drum roll please) *negative* $30,000 . . . not

THE TYPICAL AGENT STORY

my best work, but we are still chugging. I'm also not a golden child or a closet genius. My communications degree from a small liberal arts university isn't exactly a huge money-maker. In fact, my first "real" job paid me a whopping $19,500 a year. I didn't start out with money, connections, or any real professional advantages. I'm just a normal guy who wants to do business in an abnormal way.

The point is, I'm nothing special. There's a pretty big chance you're a lot smarter than I am and starting off from a much stronger position than I did. That means you, too, can do everything I've done—*and more*. Maybe your kids are older and gone, or you're young and single, or you're in your late thirties like me with young kids but struggling to figure out how to consistently and cost-effectively generate business. Maybe you're a stay-at-home mom with limited hours each day to build a business. Maybe you're a part-timer working a W-2 to pay the bills and trying to grow a side hustle into your next opportunity.

No matter your lot in life, we all want the same thing—a profitable, sustainable business that we actually enjoy and that leaves time for family, friends, and other pursuits. That's not too much to ask for, right?

But hope leaks. We start with a big bucket of hope. It takes too long to get a client, and some hope leaks out. Then, we finally get a client, and we pour some hope back into the bucket. That client tries to get out of the contract after he's cleared the home inspection and appraisal—everything that would have given him a way out—leaving him stuck in a deal he can't get out of. So, he threatens to sue the seller, sue the other agent, and "go to the papers." You get stuck in a cussing match between the buyer and listing agent. You think, *If this is what real estate is like, count me out.* Finally, both sides drop the lawsuit talk, your name isn't in the papers (whatever that would have meant), and you end up releasing the very first (and only) client you've had in your career.

Hope leaks a lot in a situation like that. Trust me, I know . . . because that's the true story of my experience with my first client.

When our hope leaks, it is easy to rush to refill our bucket with shiny objects. Hope leaks a little, so we go buy Zillow leads. It leaks some more, so we go door-knocking despite how much we hate it. It leaks again, and we start posting on social media again. Each of these things *might* play *some* role in our business, but none of them address the root cause of all the leaks:

There's a hole in your hope bucket, and it's called inauthenticity.

We need to plug the hole with authenticity and then refill the hope with pure mountain spring water—becoming more and more excellent at who we were uniquely wired to be.

You see, it's only with authentic action and personal clarity that we ever fill our buckets with the hope that we can build that life we desired by just being ourselves.

I was once listening to a speaker who was on right before me at a real estate summit. She was a branding expert. I remember her telling the audience that Dolly Parton went to sleep in her makeup so that just in case she was ever woken up suddenly, she would look the same as she always did. The speaker followed it up with, "Your job is to choose how you want to show up to people and be that every single day without fail."

I remember thinking, *How exhausting*. We are supposed to decide on an identity and forcibly show up that way every single day? Phew, I can barely make it through that sentence without needing a break. I won't mince words here: She was wrong.

You don't have to *choose* an identity and show up that way. You can *find out who you already are and become excellent at just that*. Become more and more excellent at who you were uniquely wired to be.

If anything, the easiest way to be consistent is just to be yourself, to be who you were going to show up as anyway.

If this resonates with you and you desire that level of authenticity and a restoration of hope, this book will help.

The ideas I'm sharing are meant to reconnect you to the purpose of this business. To challenge the industry standards. To call you to greater authenticity. To remind you of the proper scoreboard for success. To inspire you to create a vision for your life that only *you* control and then use the PDA Formula to achieve it.

Excited? I hope so. Too many agents are feeling the weight of inauthentic action. Too many are bogged down with bad clients and ignoring their families. Too many are waking up each day, stepping onto the hamster wheel, and chasing an unending cycle. It's time to step into something greater, my friend and fellow agent. It's time to win at work without losing at life.

part 2
The Scoreboard

What comes to mind when you think of a scoreboard? I think of all those times in high school baseball, hoping and praying we would score more runs and end up on top. I think of all the times watching a football game with the clock running out and my team down by two. I think of turning on the TV and immediately knowing who is winning and who is losing. The scoreboard, much like the scale in your bathroom, has no emotions or opinions; it just tells you facts. Are you winning or losing? Is your weight going up or coming down?

But here's the big difference between the scoreboard the industry has given us and the scoreboard at a sports stadium: *Sometimes we don't even know we stepped into a game or who controls the score.* That's what we are going to explore in this section: why the scoreboard we've been told to follow is just plain wrong and what it will take to create our own scoreboard—a much better way, a life-changing way, to measure our success.

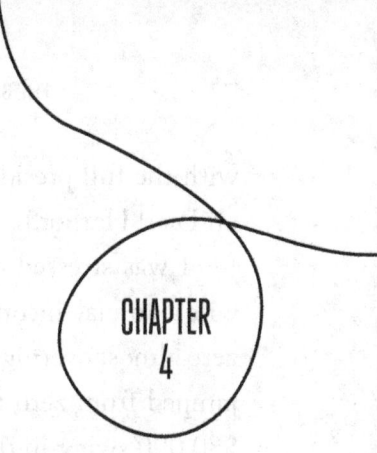

CHAPTER 4

The Industry Is Wrong

It was the spring of 2016. And I was struggling. I'd just left the team I started on and launched my own team. I'd made my first admin and agent hires, was responsible for all my own expenses, and had all my own decisions to make. Everything fell to me. That same month, a friend and I bought our first flip and unwisely decided to do most of the renovation work ourselves. What's more, my father-in-law went in for triple bypass surgery and, due to many complications, ended up hospitalized for the next two and a half years before he passed. To help care for him, my wife left her full-time job and spent most days three hours away from home with her dad.

All that happened in the *same month*—April 2016—a month which will live in infamy. (Read that with the full presidential authority of FDR reflecting on Pearl Harbor.)

I was stressed out, burnt out, and worn out. My wife's annual income had dropped from $40,000 to zero almost overnight, while my business expenses had jumped from zero to $40,000 literally overnight—an $80,000 swing in the wrong direction in one week.

Not the direction we wanted to head.

So, I did what most business owners do in this situation . . . I worked myself to death. Each day started around 7:00 a.m. in the office. I would stay there until 7:00 p.m. and then rush home to a dinner of popcorn and peanut butter (this isn't a fitness book, okay?) because my wife was with her father, and what else does a "bachelor" eat? As soon as I scarfed down my less-than-gourmet meal, I went to the house we were renovating and worked there until midnight.

That was my life Monday through Saturday.

Working 102 hours a week.

For five months straight. Lather, rinse, repeat.

I've got to admit, though, that the work was paying off. My business was doing well. We were making progress on the renovation, and my health had declined only slightly (a win in my book). Yet I knew the pace was unsustainable. I had to do something. So, I took a day off to dream a little and reconnect with *why* I was in business to begin with. Doing so energized me. I could envision a path forward out of the chaos I was living, and that felt really good.

That day off melted into a beautiful June night. In Virginia, humidity can kill a good thing quickly, but this night's humidity felt like a handmade blanket placed softly over my shoulders. Best of all, my wife was home that night, which meant I'd get a rare treat in those days: a real dinner!

Rachel and I sat down on our outdoor furniture that was begging to be replaced, and after a quick prayer, I launched into all I had been thinking about that day. I was fired up. This was the first day in a long time that I felt energized about my business. I unloaded everything I was thinking: what our business would look like in five years, how many rentals we would own, how much money we would bring in, the lake house we would have, how much money we could give to our church, and more. I just had to figure out how to sell fifty homes a year. The only tradeoff, I told her, would be the extra time I needed to work each day.

After my passionate soliloquy, my wife looked at me and said . . . nothing. She sat there, not saying a word, for what felt like twenty minutes. The silence was unbearable.

"Did you hear what I said, babe?" Confused why she had not answered, I asked her again, "What do you think?"

You know those moments in life, the pivotal moments we can look back on later as *the moment* when everything changed? This was ours.

She looked at me and said, "I love it. Let's do all of that. But instead of spending *more* time working, I want you to do it by spending *less* time working."

**"I love it. Let's do all of that. But instead of spending more *time working, I want you to do it by spending* less *time working."*

Needless to say, I was surprised—no, utterly shocked—at my wife's response. Of course, she absolutely had the right to set time boundaries for me in my work. Business is an *us* thing, not a *me* thing. As the great philosopher Homer Simpson once said to his wife, "It's uter*us*, Marge, not uter*you*."[4]

I get all my business advice from *The Simpsons* and *The Office*. I'm sure that's why I've been so successful.

Even though Rachel had the right to set those boundaries, I can still remember the thoughts that raced through my head:

Is this even possible?

Do I know anyone selling fifty homes a year under forty hours a week?

How can I generate that much business in that short of time?

Valid questions.

I realized I wasn't going to hope my way into that kind of business; I would have to *grow* my way into it, so I got to work. And with the Lord's kindness and the help of lots of learning, execution, and commitment, I sold fifty homes that year by working less than forty hours a week, and I've done that ever since.

You see, the industry is wrong. The industry tells us, "You can sell forty homes a year if you want, but it's going to cost you sixty hours a week. Or you can work less, but you will sell only twenty homes." As if we have to choose between success and no life and mild success and a life.

They say we should be proud of being open 24/7 and that "good customer service" means always answering the phone when our client needs something. All this does is create a new problem: While our clients feel cared for, our families get forgotten. Maybe we are winning at work, but we are definitely losing at life.

So, the first thing you need to know is that the industry is lying to you and it's not setting you up for the kind of success you really want. In what ways? Well...

They say you need to master all the forms of lead generation, but the truth is, you really only need to master yourself.

So, the first thing you need to know is that the industry is lying to you and it's not setting you up for the kind of success you really want.

They say it's not possible to succeed exactly how you are wired, and you need to follow a prescribed "model of a successful agent," but the problem is, you hate cold calling and all it offers you is burnout.

They say you must "do whatever it takes to succeed," but then your loved ones get left behind while you go blindly off to meet that elusive definition of success.

They say "more, more, more" and never ask "what do you want to achieve?" and then they wonder why we are exhausted and never content.

They say to grind and hustle till it hurts, yet that only leads to lost marriages, worthless vanity, and injured relationships.

I kept seeing this over and over and over again. When I first told my team leader (essentially the CEO of a Keller Williams Realty office) that I wanted to sell fifty homes in under forty hours a week, all by referral, in my second year in the industry, she literally said, "That's not possible." The person who was supposed to be encouraging and cheering on my success told me I couldn't do it. She had borrowed the narrative of the industry that success looked the same for everyone:

Be in the office at 7:00 a.m. for script practice.

Cold-call three hours a day at a standing desk with your headset on.

Wear a nice suit.

Drive a nice car.

Show homes until late at night.

Only then can you run home, squeeze in a little sleep, take a quick shower, and come back to do it all again.

That's it. That's the picture of success the industry is selling us. They say, "You can make more money than you ever imagined!" But they never say the rest of the real estate industry guarantee: "But it'll cost you your life."

The sad truth is that the industry doesn't care about us. We are just a means to its own continued existence. What we have to sacrifice along the way is irrelevant as long as we sell a lot of homes, make a lot of money, and pay our dues. As my friend and business partner Dave Caggiano likes to say, "The industry is the dairy farmer, and we are the cows in the stalls. The farmer needs to keep the cows producing milk."

Nothing illustrated this truth to me more than a speaker at Keller Williams Mega Camp one year. Mega Camp was one of the flagship events for the company, with thousands of agents in attendance. All the presenters were the best of the best in the business. This particular speaker led a team that had just sold *one thousand* homes the year before. Super impressive. She was clearly very bright, very driven, and far smarter than I could ever be. But here's what got to me . . .

At one point she started talking about the growth phase of her "mega team." It sounded like she was working insane hours to build and build and build. It worked, but that's not the problem. She made the comment, offhandedly, that "in those two years, I basically never saw my husband and daughter, but they understand now."

I remember sitting there shocked and deeply disappointed. A brokerage that upholds "God, Family, Business" was showcasing someone who really had the business part down but had seemingly no regard or regret for a whole two years that she missed her family.

I started to realize a simple yet disappointing truth about the real estate industry: All that matters to them is the number of transactions, sales volume, and Gross Commission Income (GCI). They weren't showcasing the stay-at-home mom who poured her heart into her kids and then sold ten homes a year on the side. They didn't showcase the dad who sold thirty homes a year when he could have sold fifty, because he wanted to show up at all his son's soccer games. They

THE INDUSTRY IS WRONG

didn't showcase the grandmother who spent most mornings watching her grandkids so her son could go to work. They didn't showcase anyone trying to live out a different scoreboard of success; they only showcased people who lived up to the industry's definition of success!

I do not personally know the woman who presented at Mega Camp that year. She could be an incredible wife and mom, and I truly hope she is. I also know plenty of uber-successful agents who have great family lives. Being successful in business does not mean you are unsuccessful at home; that can be true, but it certainly isn't always true.

I also know Keller Williams is not the only company that showcases the traditional view of success, so this story is in no way meant to disparage this great company or all the other great companies. I spent ten wonderful years with Keller Williams Realty and am so thankful for all I learned there.

The point is that we need to change the way the industry keeps score. Because if you change the way you keep score, you change the way you play. At the next national real estate event you attend, how refreshing would it be if the person on stage shared how they sold thirty-five houses that year while they homeschooled their kids, had a date night with their husband each week, and prioritized family movie nights on Fridays?

The truth is, every game has a score. How do you know who won the football game? You check the score. How do we know who won the NBA Finals? Check the score. Every sport has a score, and that's how we know who won. But real estate is not a sport. There isn't simply one winner and one loser, and there isn't just one way to keep score.

One of the most detrimental aspects of our industry is the curse of constant comparison. Every time an agent posts their closings from that month on social media, you wonder why you aren't doing that too. Every time you go to "Realtor prom" and get an award, you know there are lots of other agents getting a better award. When you pull up to the office in your aging Hyundai Santa Fe with a crack in the windshield (guilty) and all the cars around you are BMWs, Lexuses, and Jaguars, you feel like you aren't measuring up. But this rarely if ever motivates us, right? In fact, the quickest way for you to feel discouraged is to allow what is happening *around* you (e.g., someone else's success) to inform what should be happening *within* you.

We have to be careful and aware of the industry narrative that success is a one-size-fits-all approach and that there is one path we must all follow if we want to make it.

I remember meeting an agent who was a stay-at-home mom, which is probably the hardest job there

The quickest way for you to feel discouraged is to allow what is happening around you (e.g., someone else's success) to inform what should be happening within you.

is. Let's call her Julie. Julie had two kids at home, her husband worked, and her primary stated purpose in life was to raise and homeschool her children well. She sold real estate on the side because it was fun and something to do that provided adult interaction. Julie had sold seven homes the year before, and everyone in her office was pushing her to sell more, do more, work more. They told her she had far more potential, and she wasn't living up to it.

When I met Julie, she was stuck in this difficult, emotional place. On the one hand, she was still doing what she wanted to do—homeschool and raise her kids—but on the other hand, she continued to feel like a failure because everyone was telling her she needed to do more.

I looked at Julie and said, "You should be really proud of yourself for selling seven homes last year, but you should be even *more* proud of keeping your feet right where you want to keep them—with your kids. Build your life first, and then fit your business into that life. If that means seven homes is the maximum you can sell without giving up homeschooling, then aim for seven. If that means you could sell twelve, then aim for twelve. But never aim for anything that would require you to give up your highest priority—your family."

Julie let out this sigh of relief like someone had finally given her *permission* to live like she wanted to live. You see it, don't you? The industry keeps pushing us, crafting a narrative of what it takes to succeed simply to line its own pockets, ignoring who may get run over. How dare someone else tell us what we should accept as success.

In 2018, I hired a new coach because I wanted to become a better business owner. I had sold fifty homes, all by referral, in each of the past two years. When I first met this coach, I told her my goal was to keep selling fifty homes but to do it in less time, and that's why I wanted her help. On our very first call, she gave me homework—to cold-call three hundred people and knock on one hundred doors before our next call. Keep in mind, I had never door-knocked or cold-called before and had made it clear I had no intention to.

When she gave me that homework, I flat out said, "I'm not going to do that," to which she replied, "Then Garrett, you're not going to succeed in this industry."

I felt like I was already doing pretty well. I was in the top 1 percent of agents in my area, and I was working less than forty hours a week and doing it all by referral.

When we got on our next call, she asked if I had done my homework. I said no. She said again, more emphatically, "Then Garrett, you will never make it in this industry." Well, thankfully, she was wrong. Since then, I have sold another five hundred houses and never once have I knocked on a door or made a cold call. I did make it, and I am still making it.

My coach, my team leader, the industry itself kept trying to turn me into their ideal picture of a successful agent, but I was too stubborn to let that happen. And guess what? *I'm still standing.* (Cue Elton John.) Building my business the way I want to. Proving to you that you can do the same. The next time the industry tells you "here's what success looks like," you just smile and keep building your own life, your own way, on purpose.

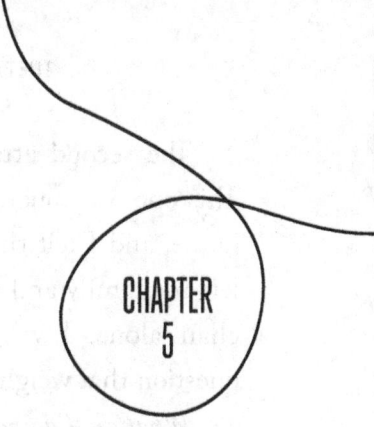

CHAPTER 5

Reclaiming an Intentional Life

In December 2023, I had my first-ever anxiety attack. I was driving our van with my wife beside me and our four kids in the back. We were headed to Colonial Williamsburg, a historic area, to walk around and enjoy some family time. Nothing out of the ordinary was happening. I was just driving along and humming to the typical kid songs we always listened to in the car, when, all of a sudden, my heart started racing, my hands started sweating, and I felt out of control. It was the strangest feeling I'd ever had.

We were on the highway on a busy Saturday. I couldn't get over to the side of the road, so I just kept driving. Thankfully, after about five minutes, it was over. But for the rest of that day, I was hyper-aware of everything going on in my body. It was scary.

The second attack came about four weeks later. This one was much worse. We were having dinner at home, and I felt this overwhelming sense of dread. I left my family and went upstairs to sit in our rocking chair alone. I was completely consumed with one question that weighed heavily on me.

What am I doing with my life?

Then I started feeling the crippling weight on my chest as I started to doubt every decision I had made and all the time I had spent building my business. It was a feeling of deep and utter despair. It's hard to explain unless you've experienced it, and I truly hope you haven't and never will. This was the first time in my life I had ever texted a friend and said, "I'm struggling, and I need help."

Why did that happen? Over the next few weeks, as I sought to understand the reason and climb out of that hole, I came to a conclusion: I was trying to do more than I was meant to do.

You see, my mom died in October 2022. She had stage four metastatic breast cancer for eight years and went downhill pretty quickly in the final few weeks. My mom was an incredible woman. Words cannot do her justice. After her passing, I spent the rest of that year thinking everything was meaningless. Why was I working? What was the point of having money? Who cared if I built a business? That led me into 2023 with a clear mission fixed in my mind: *I cannot and will not miss this time with my kids. I must build passive income because life is short.*

I went crazy. I already had my real estate team and a training business, but I also launched an Amazon business, a speaking business, and a nonprofit organization. I started writing this book, built an e-course, sold all of my stocks, and invested into cash-flowing assets. I didn't want to underreact to my mom's passing so, in truth, I overreacted.

I held everything inside myself as if I could simply grind it out. I took on everyone else's burdens but never let anyone help carry mine.

I occupied myself with way too many "priorities." I had packed my schedule too tight, pushing myself to learn new skills, succeed in new ways, expand into new arenas, and make outcomes happen no matter what—and all that work and stress and pressure eventually broke me. I was burned out. I didn't want to be around the people I normally liked being around. I held everything inside myself as if I could simply *grind it out*. I took on everyone else's burdens but never let anyone help carry mine.

In Psalm 131:1–3, King David wrote,

> O Lord, my heart is not lifted up;
> > my eyes are not raised too high;
> *I do not occupy myself with things*
> > *too great and too marvelous for me.*
> *But I have calmed and quieted my soul,*
> > like a weaned child with its mother;
> > like a weaned child is my soul within me.
> O Israel, hope in the Lord
> > from this time forth and forevermore.
>
> (ESV, *emphasis added*)

As a shepherd boy, David had gone to the front lines of a battle where his brothers and the other Israelites were fighting the Philistines. The enemy's mighty warrior, Goliath (an eight- or nine-foot mountain of a man), mocked the terrified Israelites. No one was willing to fight Goliath until David—just a teenager and probably about my size (five foot six)—boldly trusted God enough to stand up against Goliath. This scrappy kid came out of nowhere and killed Goliath with nothing but a slingshot and one smooth stone. His first shot hit the giant right between the eyes, killing him instantly. Then, to fully demonstrate God's power over Israel's enemies, the shepherd boy took a sword and cut off Goliath's head.

From that moment on, the Israelites' love for David grew, causing the Israelite king Saul to grow increasingly jealous. Saul repeatedly accused David of having ambition for the throne of Israel. He eventually went crazy and tried to kill David, chasing him into captivity. David later became king and did some incredible things for God (like writing much of the book of Psalms) and had many children, one of whom was Solomon—widely known as the wisest and richest man who has ever lived. If you want to know more, go read the book of 1 Kings in the Bible.

Okay, why am I telling a Bible story about an ancient Israelite king? Well, that backstory matters as we think about what David wrote in Psalm 131, which I quoted above. We don't know exactly what David's situation was when he wrote this psalm, but many scholars believe it was during the time Saul was hunting David down and trying to kill him. So, here is this young man, running for his life and accused of wanting to overthrow Saul to become king, and what is his cry out to God?

> I do not occupy myself with things
> > too great and too marvelous for me.
> But I have calmed and quieted my soul.

He is confessing that he is not seeking more than he is supposed to have or occupying himself with things much bigger than himself. Instead, he is trusting in the plan God has for him so he can be calm and his soul quiet. It's an amazing place for David to be in his mind and soul while facing the chaos of the world around him.

What would be the opposite of this verse? Maybe something like: "When I *do* occupy myself with things that are not meant for me, my soul is busy and unsettled—that is, I am anxious and overwhelmed."

When I sat down with my mentor about a week after my last and largest anxiety attack, he looked at me and said, "Garrett, you do not look like you're at peace." He was right, but I didn't understand. I was trying to live by the principles the industry had always taught me:

- Never settle.
- Always push for more.
- Always go bigger.
- Always level up.
- If you're not growing, you're dying.
- The only scoreboard that matters is who makes more money.

All it had brought me was anxiety, unhappiness, unfulfillment, and a battle I never stopped losing.

I'm not saying pushing for more is always a bad thing; we were made to be excellent, so we should strive for excellence. But it's important to stop and ask if you might have occupied yourself with things too great and too marvelous for you. Are you striving to be more than you were made to be? Does your soul feel at peace?

Reclaiming an intentional life starts with an honest assessment of where you are and how you're doing right now, today. So . . . how are you? Stop for a second. Seriously. Just stop. Put your phone away, close your laptop, turn off the noise, and listen to yourself.

Reclaiming an intentional life starts with an honest assessment of where you are and how you're doing right now, today.

How . . . are . . . you?

How are you *really*?

We've been trained to wear a mask most of the time. A client or coworker asks us how we're doing, and we don't hesitate to blurt out, "I'm great! It's a great time to buy a house!" It leaps out of our mouths almost on instinct, as if we must always be happy-go-lucky anytime we see someone. I'm concerned about how often this mask we wear to work gets stuck to our faces. We end up wearing it at home, with our friends, at church, and, worst of all, when we're alone.

How am I?

I'd argue that most of the time, we have no idea. No idea at all.

I once shared the idea of the mask and my concern for our industry with a group of rock star agents when one of the participants spoke up and shared a story. She started by saying how hard it was that her friends and those outside the real estate industry didn't really know her. They looked at her life and her social media, and they all assumed she was living some ridiculously amazing life, making a million a year and strolling through beautiful houses all day. She described the pressure she felt to play into that and not let them see the *real* her.

She said she was at the gym one day when a friend (outside of real estate) walked up and simply said, "Hey, how are you?" Unexpectedly, everything just poured out of her—tears upon tears because she wasn't okay. She was struggling trying to maintain an image of success, and it was killing her.

What about you?

Years ago, at a church retreat, I heard a pastor say, "God loves the *real* you, not the *ideal* you." I think that applies to how the people around us in this business see us too. Our clients want to see the real us, not the ideal us. They want authenticity (more on that later, in part 3), but we've been programmed by the industry to portray only one face—success, success, success.

Everything is not always okay; that's just the human experience. And guess what? It's *okay* to not be okay. It's okay for this to be hard. It's okay to be honest and say this has been a hard season in real estate or in your life. It's okay to be honest that you're struggling with all the demands on your time between work and family and whatever else. It's okay.

What's *not* okay? It's not okay to keep hiding, and it's not okay to do nothing about it. So, we are going to do something about it—right now.

Step 1: Get Real with Yourself

We've already discussed this, but I want you to go through a brief, ten-minute exercise right here and now. As I suggested before, put your phone away, close your computer, turn off the music, and just be still. It will take a few minutes for your mind to settle down because you're not used to stillness. Ponder just this one simple question: *How am I doing?*

Go ahead. I'll wait.

Finished? Good. Let's keep going.

Here's my challenge and encouragement to you: Right now, look at your schedule for next week and block off ten minutes to ask yourself that question again. If you don't know where you are, how will you know how to get where you want to be?

Step 2: Get Clear with Your Schedule

Next, I want you to look back into last week. If you were traveling, on vacation, at a conference, or doing anything else that was unusual, skip that one and look back at a "typical" week you had. With that specific week in mind, answer the following questions:

1. What did you do that you really *loved* doing?
2. What did you do that you really *hated* doing?
3. What did you do that *only* you could do?
4. What did you do that *someone else* could do?
5. What did you do that *served* the people you love most?
6. What did you do that *didn't* serve the people you love most?

I want you to take an honest look at your schedule. Again, we will go over authenticity more in depth in chapter 7, but for now, what did you do last week that is totally not you? Did you spend three hours cold-calling even though you hate it? Did you spend two hours making an Instagram reel even though you don't love social media and no one is going to watch it? Did you miss picking your daughter up from school because you were putting up a lockbox that someone else could have handled?

I want you to have awareness about where your time is going and the authenticity of the actions inside of that time.

Let's take a quick pause because, if you're like me, you dog-eared this page, convincing yourself you will work through the questions and steps "later," but then the later never comes . . . and neither does change. I want you to have more than new thoughts and ideas running through your head at the end of this book. I want you to be on your way to *a new life*. It takes action, not just information. So, actually stop, get quiet for a few minutes, work through the questions, and come back to the book when you are ready.

Step 3: Get Clear with Your Priorities

Now that we have a better understanding of what's really going on in ourselves and with our time, we need to gain clarity on our priorities. We will discuss this more in depth in chapter 11, "Hierarchy of Attention." For now, just know that it is easy for us to assume that, as an agent, it's our responsibility to give everyone, everywhere access to our attention all the time.

You know you need to get dinner on the table, but your client is calling. So, you stop cooking to talk about a home inspection while your kids are crying and the chicken is burning. But that's okay; you can attend to everyone's needs at the same time, right?

You know you need to be present with your spouse on date night, but a "lead" just came in. You can break away for a minute to answer the phone without putting a damper on things because "that's just how this business works," right?

The problem is, it's hard to remember our priorities and then act on them. When you don't know who or what the true priorities are in your life, everything becomes a priority. And when *everything* is a priority, then . . . well . . . *nothing* is a priority—not really. That means nothing gets the attention it deserves.

So, once again, I'm going to ask you to think through some questions.

1. *Who* do you care about most in the world?
2. *What* do you care about most in the world?
3. What, if it were *taken* away, would not really bother you?
4. What, if it were *taken* away, would devastate you?
5. *Who* in your life needs you to show up better?
6. *Where* in your life are you showing up but don't need to?

Early in my marriage, I was leading music at our church every week. Rachel told me one Sunday how hard it was for her that we never got to ride to church together because I was always getting there early to set up and staying late to clean up. But I loved leading music and didn't want to give that up, so I asked my pastor what he thought I should do. His response changed my life.

"Garrett, the church can find another music leader, but Rachel can't find another husband."

And now that I have kids, that wisdom totally applies to parenting too. The client can find another agent, but your kids can't find another dad or mom. The FSBOs (for sale by owners) can be called by someone else, but your mom can't find another son to take care of her. You get the point. Let's be clear on *who* we want to serve *most*.

Once we know who we want to serve most, what we love to do, and how we are actually doing, we can start taking action to totally transform the way we think about success and set adjusted goals for ourselves. We can finally create our own scoreboard and reclaim an intentional life.

Now let's do just that.

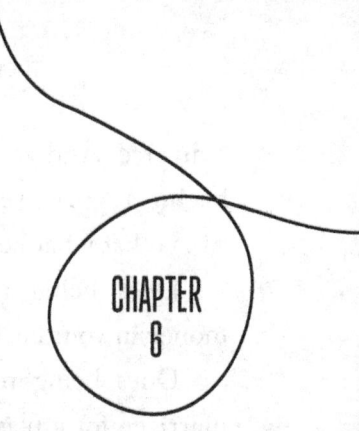

CHAPTER 6

Creating the Scoreboard

It was 2018, and I was at "Realtor prom," which I mentioned earlier. You know Realtor prom—we get dressed up all fancy, most people drink too much, and everyone gets an award from the local Realtor association.

I had sold fifty homes that year and was winning a platinum award for being in the top 5 percent of agents out of ten thousand. I remember hearing other agents talk about how awesome it would be to be the number one agent in the whole market. They aren't wrong; it would be pretty awesome. But it's only awesome *if* you can hit that mark *and* still succeed in life and at home. You see, that year, the number one agent in our market had sold a ton of houses, but his company had lost money and he'd just gone through a divorce. And yet, there he was, being celebrated for having a "great" year?

Is that what being number one looks like?

Does being number one mean actually *losing* money in your business?

Does being number one mean sacrificing your marriage for a plastic trophy and a round of applause from a group of mostly strangers?

Not to get too *churchy*, but it reminds me of an important question Jesus asked His own "top producers" in the Bible: "What good is it for someone to gain the whole world, yet forfeit their soul?" (Mark 8:36 NIV).

When we measure success in only one way, we focus on only one thing.

When we measure success in only one way, we focus on only one thing. Not anymore. By the end of this chapter, you will have a totally new way to measure success in your life. A measurement that only *you* get to influence. A definition of success that is specific to you and nobody else.

So, what is the right scoreboard? Admittedly, this is hard. I have wrestled with the concept many times, and my definition has changed over time. Remember, the heart behind this is that *you*—*not* the industry—get to choose what success looks like.

In my opinion, each scoreboard should have only three items on it:

1. Business Goal
2. Personal Goal #1
3. Personal Goal #2

That's it. And yes, to be absolutely clear, your scoreboard should not focus only on your business goals. That is a mistake way too many agents—and every other kind of professional—make way too often. Remember, the aim is to win at work *and* in life. The only way to do that is to make sure your personal goals (your life) outweigh your business goals (your work) 2:1.

You get to customize what these things look like for yourself. As for me, I have a profit goal (business), a marriage goal (personal #1), and a family goal (personal #2).

Now, it's your turn. Look back through your answers to the questions I asked you to consider in chapter 5. Think about what you would really love to do, who you want to spend more time with, and/or what would really level up your family relationships, and then write everything down. Write out your financial and transaction goal. Write out whether you want to start a team, invest, or do something special with your family. Dream a bit and write it all out.

For example, let's use my brainstorming from 2022. Here are the priorities I came up with when I asked myself those questions:

1. Make $500,000 in profit
2. Purchase two rental properties
3. Step out of production and sales
4. Have a monthly "date" with each of my kids
5. Take every Friday off
6. Take four weeks off during the year
7. Have a biweekly date night with my wife
8. Get down to 195 pounds

But it wasn't that simple. Because it is so easy for me to use the same scoreboard that everyone else uses, I was mostly focused on the $500,000 profit goal and purchasing two rental properties. So, what did I do? I added agents to my team, hired more admin, and set a goal to sell one hundred and fifty homes and make $500,000 in profit.

A few months in, I realized that the amount of time and effort it would take me to make $500,000 meant I would not be able to take Fridays off, guarantee a biweekly date night, or take four weeks of vacation with my family. It dawned on me that I simply had too many goals on my scoreboard, and those goals

CREATING THE SCOREBOARD

were competing among themselves. I had forgotten the age-old rule: When you say yes to one thing, you say no to something else.

So, I narrowed my scoreboard. I cut the list down to three things:

1. Make $500,000 in profit (business goal)
2. Take every Friday off (family goal)
3. Have a biweekly date night with my wife (marriage goal)

And that became my very first scoreboard. For the first time, I was defining what success looked like *for me*. I went back to my whiteboard and erased the three things I'd been tracking for so long: number of transactions, volume, and profit. Then, I filled the now-empty whiteboard with my new goals, my scoreboard: $500,000 profit, every Friday off, biweekly date night. For the first time, I was focused on what I *really* wanted to measure, not what the industry told me I was *supposed* to measure.

Real talk: When I created my first scoreboard in 2022, I did not hit my profit goal. In fact, I fell short by half. Some might call that a swing and a miss, but not me. I was okay with it. I realized along the way that in order to achieve my two personal goals, I would need to let go of such a huge financial goal. It wasn't because it's not possible to make that much money *and also* have freedom of time—it most certainly is possible—but because I simply didn't know yet what I needed to know to do it. So, I had to let it go.

The right scoreboard brings proper clarity and focus. When you feel like your current setup in your business or your team is off in some way, or when you are consistently feeling burnt out, check your scoreboard. Are you trying to do too much? Are your three goals compatible? Do you have the knowledge and training to accomplish your professional goal without disrupting your personal goals? Are you too focused in one area and abandoning the others?

This is why being "dollar-productive" is so important (more on that soon). If you can squeeze $50 out of every $1 you spend instead of just $10 out of every $1, you can actually work less and make more, or at least the same.

Instead of building a business and then designing a life to fit into that business, I desire for us to build a life first and then design a business to fit that life.

Who in your life is waiting for you to figure this out? Who in your family wishes they could spend more time with you but you've been chasing the wrong

CREATING THE SCOREBOARD

scoreboard this whole time? Now is the time to stop and think. Gain clarity, gain perspective, and do things purposely, not on accident.

Here's my hope for all of us: Instead of building a business and then designing a life to fit into that business, I desire for us to build a life first and then design a business to fit that life. By now you can tell I'm a fan of reflection-focused lists, so here are a few more questions designed to help you realign your priorities:

1. How much money do I *need* to make?
2. How much time each week do I want for _____? (Think: dates, kids, alone time, hobbies, etc.)
3. Who in my life needs me to be more present?
4. What can I do to show up better for them?
5. How much sleep would I like to get each night?
6. What hours do I want to work each day?
7. How much time off do I want to take this year?

Here's an example of how this can play out in your life and create clarity in your scoreboard. (I'm using my own answers):

1. How much money do I *need* to make?
    a. **$200,000**
2. How much time each week do I want for . . . (dates, kids, alone time, hobbies, whatever)?
    a. **Dates: Two or three nights per month**

b. **Kids: 8:00-9:00 a.m. each morning and 5:00–8:00 p.m. each night**
   c. **Alone time: I'm still working on this one. I have young kids!**
   d. **Read: Ten hours (this is how I rest)**
3. Who in my life needs me to be more present?
   a. **My wife and my kids**
4. What can I do to show up better for them?
   a. **Intentionally end work at 5:00 p.m. each day, take every other Friday off to have extra family time, don't work on weekends**
5. How much sleep would I like to get each night?
   a. **Eight hours would be amazing, but I'll be happy with seven**
6. What hours do I want to work each day?
   a. **9:00 a.m.–5:00 p.m.**
7. How much time off do I want to take this year?
   a. **Four weeks plus every other Friday**

Once you answer these questions for yourself, you have the raw materials you need to build the right scoreboard.

Remember, this is *your* scoreboard, so build it however you want. You can have more than three goals, but I strongly suggest keeping it simple. None of us can do ten things at the same time and nail every

CREATING THE SCOREBOARD

one of them. We've all learned that if we aim for *everything*, we won't hit *anything*. So, aim intentionally and pick intentionally. That's why I recommend only three items and no more than five.

Having the right scoreboard in place allows you to start designing a business that serves you, one that doesn't compete with your other goals but rather makes those other goals possible. You do this by asking yourself the right questions.

We'll use my scoreboard again as an example. With my three goals in place (and written on my whiteboard as a constant reminder), I can craft the key question:

> *I have only eight hours each day. I don't start until 9:00 a.m., and I'm done by 5:00 p.m. I'll have less than that every other week, since I'm taking every other Friday off. So, what kind of business allows me to work no more than forty hours a week and still earn $200,000 a year?*

We never get the right answer if we don't ask the right question. This question forces us to solve the *right problem*. That's where we want to be—forcing our minds to solve the question we created for ourselves, not one handed to us by the industry.

Let me give you a brief history lesson on the game of basketball to reinforce the power of a scoreboard. The game was invented in 1891 in Springfield,

Massachusetts, by a Canadian PE teacher named James Naismith as a way to condition young athletes during cold months. Naismith was a thirty-one-year-old graduate student when his boss asked him to create an indoor activity. The original game consisted of peach baskets (with the bottom still on, meaning the ball had to be retrieved after each score using a ladder) and a soccer-style ball. He published thirteen rules for the new game, which he called "basket ball," including:

1. The ball may be thrown in any direction with one or both hands.
2. A player cannot run with the ball. The ball can only advance by passing it to another player, who must then throw it from the same spot where he caught it.
3. A goal shall be made when the ball is thrown or batted from grounds into the basket and stays there.
4. The side making the most goals in that time shall be declared the winner.

And voilà—basketball was born.[5]

One hundred and thirty years later, are we still playing by these same rules? Not entirely. At its inception, you couldn't dribble, you couldn't shoot three-pointers, and dunking the ball into a peach basket that was nailed to the bleachers just wasn't going to happen. Would there be major TV deals for all NBA teams if they had to stand still, couldn't dunk, and had to wait around for someone to fish the ball out of a peach basket every time someone scored? If basketball hadn't evolved over time, would any of us know who Michael Jordan is?

No, of course not.

Let's put that into our professional context. Let's say James Naismith went on to create a new game called "the real estate industry." What kind of rules might he have started with? What policies and "best practices" do we put up with today, even though they feel archaic? I think it would look something like this:

1. Success requires sixty hours a week.
2. The only goal is to sell as many homes as possible.
3. You must be a master of cold-calling, door-knocking, hosting open houses, buying leads, using social media, and generating referrals. And you must always be doing all of these, all at once, all the time.
4. All that matters is the number of deals, GCI, and profit.
5. You must be available 24/7 for your clients.

6. A new lead coming in is more important than sitting down with your family for an uninterrupted dinner.
7. You only know who wins the game by endlessly comparing yourself to other agents.

If we just play this game "by the rules," we will win. That's what we are told. These are the rules. Play the game. It's that simple.

Except it's not.

What if we realized the industry was wrong? What if we rejected their rules and instead decided to create our own? *What if we decided we didn't want to be a famous basketball player (or real estate agent) but wanted to be famous at home?* What if we decided we didn't need to compare ourselves to other agents to determine who "wins" the game? What if we decided we could determine what victory looked like because it's *our* game?

When I met Pete (not his real name), he was working a normal W-2 job. He had a wife, three kids, a mortgage, and not enough money. So, he decided real estate would be a good side hustle. The good news—real estate started working. The bad news—it was consuming him. His family was making a lot more money but seeing a lot less of their husband and dad. He was missing out on soccer games, music recitals, and date

CREATING THE SCOREBOARD

nights. He was becoming more successful as a business owner and less successful as a leader of his family. He had lost sight of his scoreboard. He told his family, "I'm doing this for you," but what they were getting in exchange wasn't what they wanted at all. They didn't want more money, better vacations, and more stuff. What they really wanted was Daddy at home to tuck them into bed.

I told Pete he needed to make a choice: either go full-time into real estate or stay in his W-2, decide how many homes he actually *needed* to sell for his family, and then refer everything else out. Most importantly, I told him the decision needed to be made alongside his wife. As I've said, business is an *us* thing, not a *me* thing. Ultimately, Pete and his wife decided he would stay in his W-2 job, sell a few homes a year just to give them some cushion in their life, and happily spend more time together as a family instead of chasing some foreign definition of success.

Now, did Pete make less money than he could have? Yes.

Did he miss out on a lot of business? Yes.

But was he more successful in the way he wanted to be and his family wanted him to be than he'd been before? Absolutely yes.

I said earlier that if you change the way you keep score, you change the way you play the game. If basketball took away the three-point shot, the players would change the way they play. In the same way, if you change your personal scoreboard—your highly personalized scoring system—you will change the way you play.

When you understand the new rules of the game, your mind can start figuring out all the little solutions you probably can't see right now. Don't be scared. This is the moment you reclaim your own direction of your own business.

It's your life.

It's your business.

Take them both exactly where you want them to go.

part 3
The PDA Formula

The PDA Formula, the framework of scoreboard philosophy, stands for *Predictable, Dollar-Productive,* and *Aligned*. I designed it with real estate agents in mind, but any salesperson can use this framework to succeed in making more sales and generating more profit. After all, as the old saying goes, it's not how much you make; it's how much you keep.

This is the exact framework that allowed me to grow a successful and consistent sales funnel, build a team, step out of production, and still bring in $200,000+ a year while working fewer than five hours a week.

Now, before I dive into the PDA Formula, let's set the stage a little bit. I want you to take a moment for some internal reflection and take a snapshot of where you are *right now* in your business and life. After all, if we don't know where we started, we will never know how far we have gone or still need to go.

Ask yourself these questions:

1. What is my current lead generation framework? (e.g., three streams of leads coming in: referrals, social media, and open houses)
2. What are my most effective lead generation strategies? (the lead sources that produce the most business for you)

3. What is the financial return on each of my lead generation strategies? (revenue vs. expenses, including any broker split)
4. Do my lead generation strategies fit my personality? (i.e., did you enjoy running the Facebook ad, do you like doing open houses, do you enjoy posting on social media, etc.)

You may not know the answers off the top of your head, and that's okay. It's common for the agents I coach to not truly know the structure of their lead generation or how effective their efforts are. In fact, I've never coached anyone one-on-one who knew these answers the first time I asked them. Take a moment, ask yourself the questions, and get a snapshot of where you are today. Write something down, even if it's just an educated guess or a few words or phrases to get you started.

Next, I want you to close your eyes and allow yourself to sit still for a moment. *Make* yourself take a minute of peace and quiet. Take a deep breath in . . . then out . . . in . . . then out. Imagine knowing the exact lead generation formula that creates consistent, profitable clients. Now, imagine that you actually *enjoy* doing that thing. Think about how it feels to have clarity and direction—a singularly focused direction that has your full attention. Think about how it feels to be purposeful and confident. Think about how it feels to no longer be on the hamster wheel and moving forward intentionally. Imagine a business that offers you a life lived on purpose.

All that you are hoping for in your business is just one formula away.

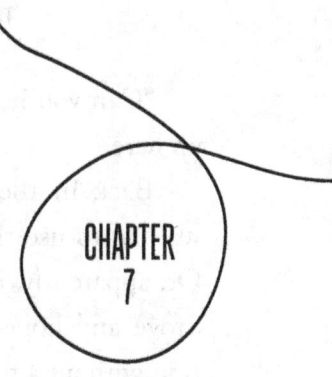

CHAPTER 7

Authenticity

"Wait, where are you?" I couldn't believe my ears. It was the Sunday before classes restarted after the fall break of my freshmen year of college.

"We just crossed into North Carolina. I think we took a wrong turn."

My friends Tatum and Beth were driving back to school and thought they had only taken a wrong turn. Nope. Instead, they had somehow passed the exit for school and ended up an hour and a half away from Christopher Newport University in Newport News, Virginia.

I laughed and said, "Uh, you somehow missed our exit on Interstate 64, got on Interstate 664, then merged onto Interstate 186. You didn't take *a* wrong turn; you took *a lot* of wrong turns."

"Can you help us? We don't know how we ended up here."

Back in the day when GPS was not common, we had to use these weird things called paper maps. Or, apparently, if you were a college student, you just drove and hoped you made it to your final destination without a real understanding of how to get there. Well, that didn't work out very well for Tatum and Beth. So, how has it worked out for you?

Have you ever taken a wrong turn in business? I know I have. How about missing an exit or just plain moving forward without even realizing you had already completely missed your destination? Have you ever ended up somewhere, looked around, and wondered how you got there and how to get back?

No, this chapter isn't about goal setting, although it could be. It certainly isn't about how to read a road map (I'm young enough that I definitely don't know how to do that). This chapter is a chance to look at your business honestly and discover where and when you made the decision to take the exit ramp and turn away from your God-given strengths, natural tendencies, and unique superpowers, and turn toward the industry's definition of success and the type of person you "need" to become. Put simply, this is about staying aligned with who you truly are and building a business around that.

AUTHENTICITY

As we get started, there are two truths you need to know:

- **TRUTH 1:** The more aligned you are with a lead generation tactic, the more consistent you will be on it.
- **TRUTH 2:** The more aligned you are with that tactic, the better you will be at it.

Put another way, the more naturally something comes to you, the better you will be at it and the more often you will do it.

I'm the anti "you've-got-to-do-it-until-it-becomes-natural-for-you" guy. I've never really bought into the idea that you can force yourself to do something you hate over and over and over again until you suddenly love it. That's never happened for me. What has worked, though, is focusing my efforts on things I actually enjoy and turning those things into effective ways to grow my business.

I've never really bought into the idea that you can force yourself to do something you hate over and over and over again until you suddenly love it.

I don't mean to imply this will be easy, though. We still have to do the work to figure out our own strengths and how we can elevate them into a business. And we obviously still need to work hard and not be defined by laziness. But I'm tired of the industry telling us we must disconnect our internal wiring and become someone that we've never actually been before in order to succeed. That's not alignment; that's submission.

Here's the easiest graph I can show you:

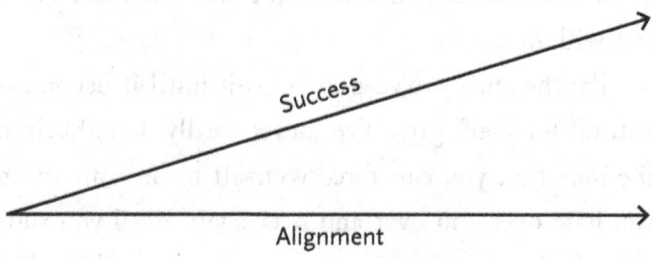

AUTHENTICITY

The greater you are in alignment with who you naturally are, the greater success you'll have. Let me give you an example.

At the end of 2021, Jesse (my team's lead agent) was wrapping up his first full year in the industry. Like me, he also worked 100 percent by referral. We were having our one-on-one weekly meeting.

"Jesse, we are going to start building your business around you being exactly who you already are," I told him.

Jesse loves to fish—so much so that he takes his boat out fishing two or three times a week. I, on the other hand, don't understand fishing. I think it's boring and would rather be napping. But Jesse was all about it. He not only loved doing it but also loved talking about it with people, even strangers. It came easy for him. It was natural. It was in his bones, his wiring. It would have been foolish for us not to incorporate what he was already doing and what he was already good at into his business. After all, *people work with you if they like you and they are like you*. It was time to let people know who he was so they could decide if they were like him too.

So, Jesse started a Facebook group called "Reel Estate," a play on fishing and selling homes. In 2022, with only forty people in the group, he closed a whopping seven deals! How? He posted about fishing. He brought some of the group onto his boat. He shared some of his fishing secrets. *He did what he normally would do, and he made $63,000 doing it.*

By encouraging this, I simultaneously gave him permission to do two things:

1. Fish during work hours and feel good about it.
2. Enjoy the way he built his business.

Whoa, wait a minute. Did I just say *enjoy* the way he built his business? You may feel a strange resistance to that concept. Something in you may argue, "That's not supposed to happen. Business should be hard and a drain and a challenge. Business should be a grind, not a pleasure. Garrett, what are you thinking?"

Who told you that's how business is supposed to be? Whoever it was, don't listen to them. They aren't describing an enjoyable business; they're describing a daily grind. And a grind sounds like burnout. A grind sounds like missing out on important moments with important people. A grind sounds like the badge of honor worn by someone who left their loved ones behind while they sought "success."

Enjoyment is the new hustle.

Say that out loud: *Enjoyment is the new hustle.* Let that sink in. Say it a few times until you start to believe it—or at least believe it's possible.

AUTHENTICITY

Find out what you love to do, crush it, and build a big business by being exceptional at being yourself. That sounds way better than what the industry tells us to do, doesn't it?

Find out what you love to do, crush it, and build a big business by being exceptional at being yourself.

The bulk of this chapter is focused on helping you get back to the core of who you are. The industry does so much to pull us into a one-size-fits-all approach to success, and somewhere along the way, we often let go of who we are and try to become who they want us to be. Well, no longer. It's time to discover who you are and be exceptional at it. It's time to bring back the joy to your work. It's time to be you again.

If you take nothing else away from this chapter, please believe and remember this one truth: *You can succeed by being yourself.*

Who Wins?

We'll start with a basic question: Who wins?

Who wins at staying underwater the longest, a fish or a world-class swimmer?

Who wins in a street race, a Lamborghini or a nine-passenger van?

Who wins in a tree-cutting competition, the guy with a chainsaw or the guy with a butter knife?

Pretty obvious answers, right? But why do they win? *Because they were doing what they were made to do.*

No matter how good Michael Phelps is at swimming, he could never stay underwater longer than a fish. The fish was made to breathe underwater. The passenger van would never beat the Lamborghini in a race. The Lambo was made for speed, while the passenger van was made for utility. And bringing a butter knife to a chainsaw fight? Come on.

You see, each of these things was made with a specific purpose in mind. When used for that purpose, they will win every time. When used outside of their purpose, they might perform pretty well, but they'll never win at the highest level. It's the difference between Michael Jordan on the basketball court and Michael Jordan on the baseball field. Sure, he could do both, but he was nowhere near as successful or impressive on the diamond as he was on the court. Jordan was wired for basketball. Tiger Woods was wired for golf. Lionel Messi was wired for soccer. Simone Biles was wired for gymnastics. These athletes are legends because they played the sport they were made for and became excellent at it.

AUTHENTICITY

Would a cherry taste good in soup? Probably not. But it tastes delicious in a pie. How about a pepperoni? Would it taste good in a fruit salad? Probably not. But it's delicious on a pizza. You get the point.

This is what I want for you. Play the lead generation game you were made for. Stick to that lane and become an expert at it.

When you align, you succeed.

When the Industry Pushes Back

In 2016, I was in my second full year in the business and part of the Agent Leadership Council in my office. The ALC (as it was known) comprised six agents in the top 20 percent of that individual office. I was twenty-eight years old and had just sold twenty-seven homes the year before, all by referral. I was by far the youngest person in the room and the newest to the business. The average agent there was over forty, had been in the business at least seven years, and had sold more than forty homes the year before. I was the eager beaver; they were the sages. We were having our kickoff meeting for the year and had moved into the portion on goal setting.

I remember that moment so vividly because it changed everything for me. Our team leader (essentially the office's CEO) asked us, "What is your goal for the year?" We went around the room, and everyone shared their goals. I was last. When it came to my turn, my answer was simple.

"I want to sell fifty homes this year 100 percent by referral."

You know what I heard?

"You can't do that. You need other ways to generate business."

As you may recall from chapter 3, the team leader even laughed and said, "That's not possible. What else will you do?"

Immediately, in a room of peers who were supposed to cheer me on and a team leader whose job was to support and encourage the agents, I was told, in no uncertain terms, to let go of the method that most aligned with me.

"You need at least three legs of your business. You cannot just work by referral and sell that many."

I was being *told*, not encouraged or guided, to add lead generation efforts that were counter to my personality. Let that sink in for a moment. I was only in my second full year. I had just sold twenty-seven homes by referral, and I told them I wanted to essentially double that. Their immediate reaction was to tell me no, to fit into the industry, and to do what they say. That's the only path to success.

Have you heard that or felt it too?

AUTHENTICITY

Fortunately, I was young enough and stubborn enough to disregard their comments. That year, I went out and sold exactly fifty homes, all by referral. In fact, to this day, I've never made a cold call, bought a lead, done an open house, door-knocked, or called a FSBO. I have only ever worked by relationship, and even though I did not grow up in the area and started with only forty people in my database, I have sold more than six hundred and fifty homes in just ten years. My deep alignment with who I am and how I was wired has led to extraordinary success. It can for you too.

I should clarify something I just said. I have, in fact, made *one* cold call in my career. Just one. It went something like this . . .

"Hi, is this Mr. Smith?"

"No, I don't want to sell my house with an agent. Stop calling!" Click. The line went dead.

I called back.

"Sorry, Mr. Smith, it seems we somehow got disconnected. I was wondering if you had considered selling your home with an agent."

"Never call me again!" CLICK!

Somehow, I could actually *hear* the exclamation point of the *click* the second time he hung up on me.

I still don't remember why I made that cold call. Maybe I just wanted the full real estate agent experience of intruding on a stranger, making them angry, and having them hang up on me. I remember sitting there with the phone in my hand, thinking, *Nope. I'm never doing that again.*

And I never did.

It was my one and only cold call. Not only did it remind me why I never wanted to build my business that way, but it made me dig even deeper to master the way that aligned with me. I'll say it again: There is the industry's way of doing things, and then there is the way *you* want to do things. Figure out what that is, and then stick to it.

But how?

The Alignment Test

I was in Maryland in 2019, teaching on my Perfect 36 Touch System (a common name for a lead generation system built on referrals from the people you already know in your sphere of influence). The room was pretty full, with around fifty attendees. I was an hour into my two-hour presentation when I delved into the nuts and bolts of the system (which you will get in chapter 10 when I share my personal PDA Formula). As I was speaking, a woman in the back of the room started crying. In fact, she was full-on weeping. I didn't think my presentation was so bad it would make people cry,

AUTHENTICITY

so I paused the class and said, "In no way do I want to put you on the spot, but are you up for telling us why you are crying?"

She stood up and said, "I have been in this business for a year. I am really relational, but everyone told me I had to cold-call to succeed. Every single day, I come here and make cold calls for two hours a day. I hate it, and it's never worked. This is the first time I believe I can build a business the way I want to."

It was moving for the whole class and certainly moving for me. She wasn't hearing my system on how to generate more referrals. She was hearing, for the first time, that she had permission to build a business exactly the way she wanted to—in alignment with herself, not with someone else. This is what I desire for you.

How do we know if we are in alignment? You may immediately know the answer to this, but if not, I want you to take a moment and chew on some questions—a quick alignment test, if you will. Ask yourself:

1. *Do I like how I currently generate business?*
2. *Does my work bring me energy or drain my energy?*
3. *Am I following the crowd or maximizing my own unique superpowers?*

If you don't like your current lead generation habits, you're not in alignment.

I'll pause and reiterate that you shouldn't associate *difficulty* with *unalignment*. It can be and often is hard to do work that aligns with who we are. Building relationships is hard. Discipline is hard. Acting with integrity is hard. Perfecting your sales pitch is hard. The question shouldn't be, *Is this difficult?* The real question that matters is, *Does your current lead generation method fit you?*

If your work drains your energy all the time, you're out of alignment. If you are like that sweet woman from Maryland, coming in and doing what someone else tells you to do every single day, even though you don't like it, you're not in alignment. (I do admit there is a time and place for doing something you don't love to do just to get your business off the ground, but do that *only* until your business is off the ground. As soon as possible, switch your business into alignment.)

It's very possible that parts of you are in alignment and parts of you are not. Maybe you cold-call, door-knock, generate referrals, and host open houses, and only two of the four align with who you are. Ask the three questions above for each lead generation method you use.

AUTHENTICITY

How many times have we heard, "The joy is in the journey, not the destination"? Yet, as business owners, we only ever consider the destination. We tell ourselves to suck it up and make the calls because we have to sell the houses and make the money. Sometimes that's true—but not always. If the joy is in the journey, the journey must align with what we enjoy.

Let me say a bit more about each of the three questions before we move on.

Question 1: Do I like how I currently generate business?

I cannot tell you the number of times I have asked agents how they generate business and heard them say, after listing all their methods, something like, "But I don't really like any of it."

It's amazing how easily we concede our desire to build a business the way we want to just because we were told that's not how it's done. If I had come into the industry and started cold-calling and door-knocking, I would have hated it. I not only would have hated it but also would have been terrible at it. I can't imagine sitting there while people hang up on me angrily over and over. I tried it one time, and it tore me up for the rest of the day. I should probably have eaten a donut and taken a nap just to recover!

If I had resigned myself to a career spent working against my natural tendencies, I not only would have had poor results but very likely would not even be in this industry anymore. Operating out of alignment brings lower profits, more frustration, and higher burnout. Why would we think this is a good way to go about our work?

Knowing all this, I'll ask again: Do you like how you currently generate business?

Question 2: Does your work bring you energy or drain your energy?

I have my coaching clients do a time-and-energy audit to find out the answer to this question. First, here's how the time audit works:

1. Pick three consecutive working days.
2. During those three days, stop every thirty minutes and write down what you just did. (I suggest starting from the moment you wake up to when you end your working day.) For example, at 11:00 a.m., you might stop and write, "Checked emails and called a mortgage lender" or "Wrote notes to my database."

Here is a more detailed example:

Time	What I Just Did
9:00-9:30 a.m.	Checked Facebook and emails
9:30-10:00 a.m.	Responded to texts, called a lender
10:00-10:30 a.m.	Called a buyer, spoke about inspection
10:30-11:00 a.m.	Scheduled home showings
11:00-11:30 a.m.	Wrote notes to my database
11:30-12:00 p.m.	Checked email and posted on Instagram
12:00-12:30 p.m.	Had lunch

3. At the end of those three days, circle anything that actually produced money. Focus on lead generation efforts, not going on appointments that are a result of those lead generation efforts. For the scenario above, you would circle "Wrote notes to database" and "Posted on Instagram." Responding to texts or scheduling showings are *by-products* of lead generation, not an *action* of lead generation.
4. Be honest with yourself. This exercise is just for you, so there's no point making it look any better or worse than it really is.

When my coaching clients do this, they're usually shocked at how little time they spend actually pushing their business forward. This is the first step to maximizing your time and your alignment—understanding where your time goes.

Then, we level up the experience by understanding where our *energy* goes. Here's how to do the energy audit on top of the time audit:

1. Write next to each thirty-minute block a plus sign (+), minus sign (-), or circle (letter O).
2. A "+" means that the activity gave you energy.
3. A "–" means it drained your energy.
4. An "O" means it did not change your energy.

Let's add this column to the time audit example above:

Time	What I Just Did	Energy Result
9:00-9:30 a.m.	Checked Facebook and emails	-
9:30-10:00 a.m.	Responded to texts, called a lender	O
10:00-10:30 a.m.	Called a buyer, spoke about inspection	-
10:30-11:00 a.m.	Scheduled home showings	+

11:00-11:30 a.m.	Wrote notes to my database	+
11:30-12:00 p.m.	Checked email and posted on Instagram	-
12:00-12:30 p.m.	Had lunch	O

In our example, we can see that checking emails, talking about home inspections, and being on social media drains our energy. The excitement of scheduling showings gives us energy, as does writing notes. Responding to texts and talking to a lender doesn't change our energy, nor does eating lunch.

Why does this audit matter? So much of the work we do drains our energy or, at best, doesn't change it at all. Very little of our work is actually life-giving. For most of my coaching clients, their biggest drains are centered on lead generation—making cold calls, hosting open houses, and doing social media. The biggest energy gains for most of them center on relationships—client coffee dates, client events, meeting a lender in person, or simply engaging other humans in real conversation.

Success takes at least 80 percent of us each and every day, yet most of us show up with maybe 60 percent. How do we expect to succeed when we willingly submit ourselves to energy-draining activities? We are fighting a losing battle, running in a hamster wheel.

So, how do we use this energy audit practically and start most days at 80 percent or better?

First, you must start paying attention to trends in the categories and activities that bring you energy or drain your energy. Once you see the trends, take two actions:

1. **Minimize the time spent on the draining activities and maximize the time spent on energizing activities.** If client coffees fire you up, do them as often as you can. If checking email drains your energy, limit it to once in the morning and once in the afternoon. For each activity, ask yourself, *Is this activity truly necessary?* If it's not, find a way to get rid of it or delegate it to someone else.
2. **Pay attention to when you are at your best during the day and when you may feel a little sluggish.** For example, I am often much more energetic in the morning, so that's when I do the activities that drain my energy, like checking emails, responding on social media, and scheduling meetings. The afternoon is when I often feel a little sluggish, so that's when I schedule the activities like podcasting, writing, and coaching that fire me up. I know these activities energize me, so I intentionally

schedule them for the times when I know I need an energy boost.

It can seem counterintuitive to schedule draining activities during your peak energy and energizing activities during your low energy, but I am convinced this is the right approach. Why? Because I believe we should strive to be excellent in all we do, and if we cannot be excellent, we shouldn't do it. If I attempt a draining activity at a time of low energy, there is a 0 percent chance I will do it with excellence. If I schedule a draining activity at a time of peak energy, there is at least a 50 percent chance I will do it with excellence. If I tackle an energizing activity in low energy there is still an 80 percent chance I'll do it with excellence because the activity itself causes me to bring my A game. I'm just playing the odds of being excellent in all things.

The energy audit allows us to understand our time and our energy and use it as effectively as possible. And guess what? The activities that give you life are those that align with who you were created to be. Let me say that again: The activities that fire you up and energize you are the activities that align with who you are. There's your alignment.

And since we want to act in alignment, here is the big goal: Spend 80 percent of your time on the "+" side of energy and only 20 percent on the "-" side. Imagine how different your business and your life would be if you intentionally spent 80 percent of your day on the things that most align with who you are and how you like to work.

So again, does your work *bring* you energy or *drain* your energy?

Question 3: Am I following the crowd or maximizing my own unique superpowers?

This one is simple yet profound. Did you *choose* what to do or were you *told* what to do? Did you go willingly or begrudgingly into the work? Right before you go into your lead generation session, what emotions are you feeling? Of course, no matter how much your business aligns with your wiring, there will still be days you don't feel like doing the work, making that call, or posting that video. Life isn't perfect. But more often than not, is the work you're doing what you would choose to do?

I was sitting with another agent on the team in the office early in my career. He was even newer to real estate than I was. He had a good personality and decent sales skills, and his wife was a nurse and knew a ton of people. He had a huge network of potential clients at his fingertips. There was only one problem: He wasn't thinking about the relationships; instead, he had gone to a class on cold-calling and thought that would be his ticket to success.

He was on the phone that day, power-dialing through internet "leads." His headset was on and he, quite frankly, looked miserable. Every day for weeks, he had spent hours on the phone while I sat at my desk thinking about how I could grow the relationships I already had. When he finally got someone on the phone, their conversation went like this:

Agent: "Hi, this is Derek with Keller Williams Realty. I saw you registered on our website and you were thinking about buying a home, is that correct?"

Potential Client: "How did you get this number?"

Agent: "Well, you registered on our website. Are you looking to buy a home?"

Potential Client: "No, I'm not. Maybe in another year."

Agent: "Another year? Why not just buy now?"

Potential Client: "Listen, I'm *not* interested. I'm going to wait."

Agent: "Well, that doesn't make sense. You're making a bad decision. You should buy now . . ."

Click.

The agent turned to me and said, "That woman was terrible. She had no idea what she was doing."

I responded, "Maybe you could have approached her more gently."

He huffed and said, "No, she was just dumb and didn't do what I told her to."

Needless to say, that agent failed out of the business within three months. I don't know if he would have succeeded had he focused on a different form of lead generation (his people skills obviously needed some work), but I do know one thing for sure: The path he chose of cold-calling gave him the absolute lowest-percentage chance of success. He wasn't cut out for it. It was counter to his personality, and he wasn't good at it. Sadly, that's an all-too-common story in our industry.

Hopefully by now you know whether your current business is in alignment with you or not. I don't want you, like my cold-calling former teammate, to fail simply because you're playing a losing game. I want you to be true to yourself and become excellent at being *you*.

I would guess that most of us are out of alignment and need an adjustment. Maybe a good crack from the business chiropractor can do the trick.

The Opportunity Zone

I recently coached a woman in La Jolla, California, who was, to put it mildly, highly relational. And I mean, *highly* relational. She *loves* talking to people.

AUTHENTICITY

She will talk all day. She loves people so much that she could probably pull a Pinocchio and turn a doll into a real boy just so she has someone to talk to. As we unpacked her business, it became clear that her top sources of leads were *sphere of influence* (the people she knew) and *open houses*. That made sense because those were about relationships, where she thrives and what she was made for.

I remember her sharing with me an opportunity she had. "Garrett," she said, "what do you think about this? A lender told me I was the number one agent in this zip code. I didn't know that. So, I'm planning to send some mailers and write some notes to everyone in that zip code."

I replied, "First of all, congratulations! That's awesome that you are number one. But let me ask you a question. Does this opportunity align with how you have generated all of your other leads?"

"Well, no," she admitted, "but don't you think it's a good opportunity and something I should do?"

I said, "Lots of ideas are good opportunities, but you should say no to most of them. If we spend too much time saying yes to every 'good' opportunity that comes our way, we quickly realize our life and business have become dominated by things we said 'yes' to that we should have said 'no' to."

I could tell no one in the industry had ever told her this before.

"The first question you should ask yourself," I continued, "is, *Is this a good opportunity?* This mailing effort might pass that test. But then you've got to ask, *Is this an opportunity that I should do?* We tend to skip this second question.

"If we think it's a good opportunity, then we say yes because we don't want to miss it. But I'd argue that most of the time, these don't turn out to be *opportunities* after all; they turn out to be *distractions*."

"Okay, that makes sense," she conceded, "but how do I know which ones are distractions and which ones aren't?"

"Let me explain your personal opportunity zone. We have done the work to determine what aligns with you—face-to-face communication, specifically, open houses and sphere of influence. This is your highest and best opportunity because it's just who you are. Anything inside of your alignment circle is your *opportunity zone*, and anything outside of your opportunity zone can be a great opportunity but it's not in alignment, which makes it more of a distraction. So, your goal should be to say yes to anything that's inside your opportunity zone and no to anything that's not."

AUTHENTICITY

Example: Her Opportunity Zone

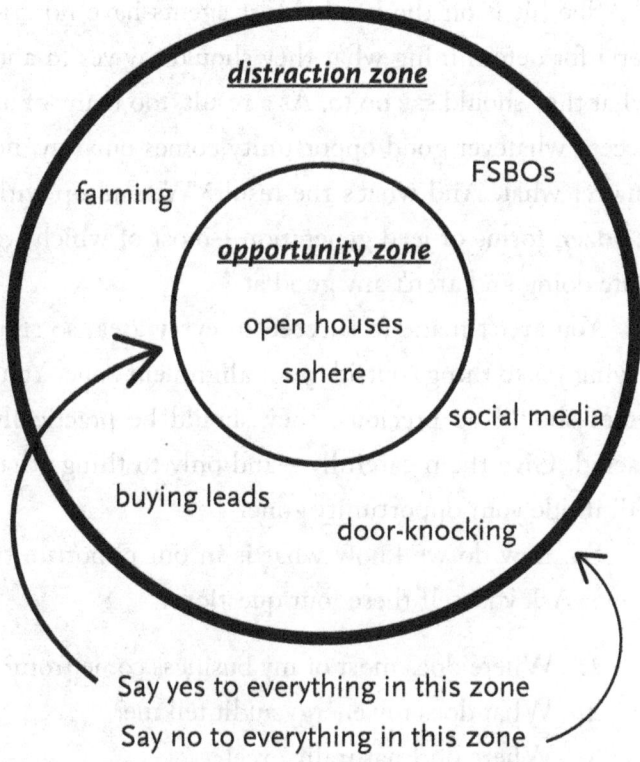

Go to www.thebalancedbreakthrough.com/zones to download your own opportunity zone chart.

I could sense the relief in her voice as she said, "That makes perfect sense. The truth is, I don't think I ever know what I should say no to and what I should say yes to. So, I say yes to everything. I feel pulled in too many directions. It's exhausting. It's nice to have a tool and some context for making those decisions."

She hit it on the head. Most agents have no criteria for determining what they should say yes to and what they should say no to. As a result, too many of us accept whatever good opportunity comes our way, no matter what. And what's the result? We end up with a dozen forms of lead generation—most of which we hate doing and aren't any good at.

You aren't made to succeed in every area, so stop saying yes to things outside your alignment zone. Your yeses should be precious; they should be practically sacred. Give them carefully—and only to things that fall inside your opportunity zone.

So, how do we know what is in our opportunity zone? Ask yourself these four questions:

1. Where does most of my business come from?
2. What does my energy audit tell me?
3. Where do I naturally excel?
4. What do I want to do?

Go ahead, answer the questions. You should clearly see your opportunity zone take shape.

The president of my alma mater, Paul Trible, used to say, "When you align around a common goal, you grow. But when you align hearts and minds, you soar."

AUTHENTICITY

As a college kid who was more interested in video games than life lessons, I never understood what he meant. But I get it now. If you're outside your opportunity zone, you can still grow toward your goal. Unfortunately, that growth is dangerous because you're growing toward your goal but losing yourself along the way. But—and this is a big *but*—if we can align our work with our hearts *and* our minds, we will soar. We will achieve our goal *and* grow ourselves. We will win at work without losing at life.

I hope you are starting to see how understanding your opportunity zone and when to say yes and knowing your scoreboard start to work together. If you are saying yes too often and to too many "opportunities," you are unable to achieve the personal goals inside your scoreboard. So the scoreboard also acts as a decision-making tool for your yeses and your noes.

Understand Thyself

At the beginning of understanding alignment is an understanding of self. Don't worry, we aren't going to get that deep and philosophical, but we do need to understand who we are and who we were wired to be. When I've taught this PDA Formula, it is common for agents to come up to me and tell me they are out of alignment. But when I ask what *is* in alignment, they aren't sure.

The problem is that we don't know ourselves very well. We've allowed those around us to dictate our actions, and we no longer even know our natural tendencies.

So, how do we start gaining an understanding? First—and I know I've asked you to do this before—I want you to pause and be still. That's right, shut off the computer, turn your phone to silent, close the music app, get in a quiet space, and just sit. Allow yourself to be still and breathe. Give yourself five minutes of silence. Ask yourself one question over and over: *What do I love to do?*

Keep sitting, even if your thoughts start running wild. For an entrepreneur, "quiet time" is one of the loudest moments of the day because our brains don't know how to chill out. But hang on. Focus. Fight through the noise and force yourself to wrestle with the question, *What do I love to do?*

Do it. Now. You've got five minutes . . .

What I've found in these moments is that eventually, something sticks out to me. It comes to the top of my mind. It may even make me smile as I think about what I love doing. And if it doesn't come to you this time, that's okay. Try again tomorrow and keep trying until you get it. You will start to recognize yourself again, and that's a beautiful moment.

The Question Mind

One of my buddies, Jake Dixon of The Locker Room, a real estate coaching organization, taught me the concept of a *question mind*. Many of us are familiar with the concept of a *mastermind*—you have one question that needs an answer, and you come up with as many ideas and thoughts on how to solve that problem as possible until you have an acceptable solution. Well, a *question mind* is the complete opposite—and far more powerful.

As the saying goes, you'll never get the right answer if you don't ask the right question. That's what makes a question mind so effective. Instead of having a problem and offering solutions, as you would in a mastermind exercise, you start with a question and, for ten minutes, all you can do is ask *more* questions. Seriously. No answers, just questions. For ten minutes.

When the ten minutes are up, you go back through all the new questions you wrote down and decide which question is the one that *truly* needs to be answered. Take that question, write it at the top of the next page, and then spend time (I suggest at least thirty minutes) journaling and processing the answer. In this way, the question mind prepares you to do the mastermind, which makes it much more effective.

Here's an example from my own life. I did this exercise for myself because I lacked clarity on where exactly

I wanted to spend my time. So, I started with the question, "What do I really want to do?" and spent ten minutes writing more questions down as they came to me.

> What do I really want to do?
> What feels like it's in my way?
> What am I doing that I don't want to do?
> What should I be doing?
> Where can I create the most impact?
> Where should I leverage?
> What do I need to do to get to the goal?
> What is the goal?
> What is my ideal life?
> What is my ideal day?
> What am I trying to accomplish?
> ✓ How am I really?

You can see the power of this first step. I *thought* the question I needed to answer was, "What do I really want to do?" I *learned* the real question was, "How am I, really?" I thought I was simply lacking clarity on what to do, but if I had only answered that initial question, I would have been treating a symptom and not the disease. This is exactly what we do so often in our

AUTHENTICITY

business. The question mind forced me to look deeper and keep asking questions until I got to the right one.

Now that I had the right question, I could start seeking the right answer. To do that, I spent the next half hour trying to answer that question. And let me tell you . . . it was not easy. This is very vulnerable for me to share, but I sincerely hope it will encourage you.

How Am I?

I'm Tired

I'm a little defeated

I feel like I'm locked to work — like I should have more ~~freedom~~

I feel like I added too much to my plate before I capitalized on what I already had

I feel like my mind is too many places

I feel like I could be a better dad and husband

I'm discouraged that I lack clarity

I feel like I don't have enough space to think

I'm prioritizing ~~work~~ speed of business over my family too much

I feel like I'm just doing things for no reason other than I can and they will work

I feel like I'm distracted by what the world has to offer

Too often, we spend time asking the wrong question and then get frustrated when we keep coming up with the wrong answer. That's like treating a headache when you have a broken leg. The question mind allowed me to get deep enough to ask the right question, the one that mattered, the one that really needed to be answered. It turned out that the problem I was facing wasn't because I didn't know what I wanted to do; it boiled down to the fact that I was hurting, and I hadn't slowed down long enough to address what was rapidly becoming physical, mental, and emotional burnout.

It can be scary to drill down into our own thoughts. I get it. But it's much scarier to live a whole life inauthentically because we are too afraid to figure out who we truly are. Don't fall for all the distractions the industry sells us as solutions. Find out who you really are and become excellent at it. That's alignment. Stop trying to work to *create* your identity. Start trying to work *from* your identity.

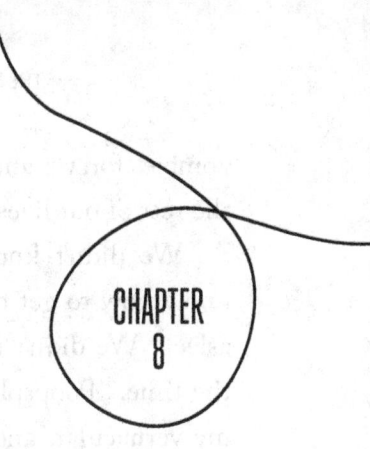

CHAPTER 8

Predictability

It was another middle of the night wake-up. I sat down on the bed next to my wife exhausted and defeated. I looked her in the eyes and said, with full conviction, "I think we ruined our lives."

Our newborn Haddie (our first child, born in 2017) had woken up crying again. Her screams filled the hallways every hour as she refused to bask in the glory of a full night's sleep. And for some reason, a baby's cry is the one sound in the world that cuts right through every other sound.

We were three weeks into parent life, and I was convinced it was all over. What had we done? Life as we knew it was kaput. I know that's dramatic, but it's absolutely how we felt. Were we destined to be walking zombies forever and sleep in three-hour increments for the rest of our lives?

We didn't know how to be parents. We didn't know how to get our daughter to fall asleep and stay asleep. We didn't understand why she was crying all the time. "Poopsplosions" had become a new word in my vernacular, and exhaustion took on a whole new level. There's *tired*, and then there's *parent tired*. Totally different. Everyone who told us to get a dog because "it will be good practice" must also think Thin Mints make you thin. Nothing—and I mean *nothing*—could have prepared us for this. We simply did not know what to do to get our desired result: a sleeping and peaceful baby.

It's amazing how many parents let out a sigh of relief after I share our struggles with our first baby. I've been told countless times, "Yes! We totally felt that way too, but I didn't know it was okay to admit it." Parenting is really tough. New transitions and changes are really tough. Sleeplessness is really tough. It's obviously why I'm no longer beautiful . . . bye-bye, beauty sleep. Well, it's either that or the donuts.

For the record, I no longer believe we ruined our lives, and I absolutely love my kids. I know now that we just had a really tough transition into parenthood.

Starting a career in real estate is often just as difficult of a transition. We get into the business because we "love helping people." Then, we have a difficult client and realize that maybe we don't love people as much as we thought. Then comes the recognition that this business isn't about people as much as it is about lead generating *for* people. It's a shock to the system. We thought the business was *serving* people, not *finding* them.

We often don't know how to "get the baby to sleep" and achieve the desired outcome, so we try any and all methods of lead generation available to us. Even when something does work, we have tried so many methods that we are no longer even sure which one of them actually paid off.

I always ask my clients early in our coaching relationship, "Where did your business come from last year?" Ninety percent of the time, they do not know the answer. The conversation normally goes like this:

Me: "How many transactions did you do last year?"

Client: "Um, I think around twenty."

Me: "And where did those twenty come from?"

Client: "Let's see. Some came from my sphere of influence, some from open houses, some from the internet, and some I don't remember."

Me: "What was your best source of leads?"

Client: "I think it was probably my sphere of influence."

Me: "Okay, and what did you do to generate those leads?"

Client: "Gosh. Honestly, I'm not really sure."

Sound familiar? Most agents do not know their business. They have no idea which actions produced which outcomes or even which lead sources produced which leads. I would compare most agents' lead generation efforts to the "everything but the kitchen sink" meal. You know the one: You've got too much in your fridge that you need to get rid of, so you mix it all together, measure nothing, and hope for the best. That's the typical lead-gen plan for the typical agent. Throw everything into a pot and see what comes out. If what emerges tastes good, you do it again. All of it. Hoping that whatever worked last time will work next time.

But you're not a typical agent, right?

Hope is not a business plan, and lead generation is no game of chance. It is a predictable result of a repeatable effort.

This approach may work for the cook at your local truck-stop diner, but you are fine dining. The chef at a five-star French restaurant doesn't operate the same way. They know exactly how much of which ingredients will create a delicious chocolate soufflé every time.

So how do we become the chef and create delicious lead generation meals over and over again? How do we make our lead generation *predictable*? Hope is not a business plan, and lead generation is no game of chance. It is a predictable result of a repeatable effort, just like the French pastry chef's chocolate souffle recipe.

Predictable. Repeatable. Delicious.

The Recipe

The first step in creating predictable lead generation is simple: *Pay attention to what you are doing.*

How often do you finish your day and think, *What did I even do today?* How often do things go unnoticed in your world because you are too distracted or moving too quickly to notice the world happening around you? How much time did you spend on social media? How much time did you spend chatting it up with other agents at the office? How much time did you spend lead generating? Start paying attention. As Nir Eyal says in his book *Indistractable,* "Everything is either a distraction or traction."[6]

One of the best ways to gain awareness is through a time audit. We went through this exercise together in the previous chapter. Go back and look at your time log. Where is your time actually going? How much of your time pushed your business forward? You cannot achieve without focus, and you cannot focus without awareness. Gain awareness; it will help you achieve more consistently.

The second step to building a predictable business is *making a lead generation recipe*. A recipe is written, duplicatable, and delivers a predictable result every time.

If you don't know how to bake a cake, what do you do? You Google a cake recipe and follow it to the letter: measure the ingredients, stir, preheat the oven, put it in to bake, and voilà! Out comes a cake.

If you enjoy that cake, then you save the recipe, and *boom*! Now you have your new cake recipe. When you need to bake a cake again, you pull up that same recipe and get to work. If you follow the recipe, bake the cake, and the taste is not quite right or even way off, then you don't use that recipe anymore. You search for a new recipe or try tweaking a few ingredients and/or the amounts, stir, bake the cake again, and test the result. That's the process until you get it just right.

What you *wouldn't* do is bake a cake you don't like and then keep baking that same bad cake again and again because the recipe says it's *supposed* to be good. It may be a great cake to some people, but that doesn't matter if you hate the taste of it. It wouldn't make sense to keep force-feeding that same bad cake to yourself and your family, would it?

Well, guess what? It doesn't make sense in business either. But isn't that what we do when we keep force-feeding ourselves the same bad recipe the industry hands us when we start out?

The key is to not just find any old recipe but to find the one that works best for *you*, one that produces the results you want in a way that doesn't make you want to bang your head against your desk for eight hours a day.

What you don't do is find a recipe that produces a terrible-tasting result but just keep using it anyway. That wouldn't make sense in the kitchen or at the office.

In my house, I'm the breakfast guy. Why? Because I'm terrible at following recipes. The few times I make dinner, it's absolutely shocking how often I have to check the recipe to remember what I'm supposed to do. Shocking and embarrassing. But with breakfast, I know how to make the perfect "daddy waffle," as my kids call them. Because I have tried different combinations and found the flavor I wanted, I can recreate the daddy waffle every time. (Since I know you'd like to steal it: 1 cup Kodiak cakes, 1 scoop Clean Simple Eats Brownie Batter protein, 1 cup whole milk. Top with no-sugar whipped cream and Walden Farms syrup, and *mmm mmm* that's good. Delicious and mostly nutritious.)

Is it so surprising that when I don't follow a recipe, the food comes out quite *un*delicious? (Is that a word? It should be.) But when I follow a tried-and-true recipe, it comes out super yummy every time.

Likewise, too many agents think they can get by on personality and wit alone in this industry without following a simple recipe. That is just not true. A predictable business requires a predictable recipe.

So, I want you to create your own lead generation recipe. And I want you to bake that "lead-gen cake" over and over until you have the perfect recipe that produces a predictable, repeatable, and delicious cake (sales). The process is very simple: Start by finding or creating your own recipe. Follow the recipe to the letter, bake it, and taste the result.

Let's dig in to some of the different real estate recipes you could try:

Recipe #1: Social Media

Most of us believe that social media is a necessity in our business, but very few of us actually want to live on social all day every day. However, since we've been told we *must* do it, we half-heartedly post and become "influencers" . . . to the thirty agents in our office and our parents. We try posting a little more often, but it delivers only meager and wildly sporadic results that offer no tangible benefits for our business, so we give up. An influencer we are not.

What if we instead created a recipe, baked the cake, and tasted the result? What if we had a simple, repeatable, written plan to follow? Here's an idea of how that could look on social media:

The Instagram Lead Generation Recipe (let bake for thirty days):

- **Ingredient 1:** Post one personal video a day showing your family.
- **Ingredient 2:** Make one real estate–related post a day.
- **Desired Outcome:** One new signed buyer client.

There you have it—an Instagram lead generation recipe. All you have to do now is execute and track.[*]

The table shows a simple way to track your social media recipe. Did you post the personal video and the business post? Good work! You are well on your way to creating a *predictable* source of generating business. Now, pay attention to the results and draw conclusions. How many views did the video/post

---

[*] Go to thebalancedbreakthrough.com/track to get your own recipe tracker.

Day 1	Tracker	Day 2	Tracker	Day 3	Tracker
personal video	yes	personal video	yes	personal video	yes
business post	yes	business post	yes	business post	yes
# of views on personal video	100	# of views on personal video	150	# of views on personal video	41
# of engagements on business post	20	# of engagements on business post	10	# of engagements on business post	23
Day 4	Tracker	Day 5	Tracker	Day 6	Tracker
personal video	yes	personal video	yes	personal video	yes
business post	yes	business post	yes	business post	yes
# of views on personal video	100	# of views on personal video	150	# of views on personal video	41
# of engagements on business post	20	# of engagements on business post	10	# of engagements on business post	23
Day 7	Tracker	Day 8	Tracker	Day 9	Tracker
personal video	yes	personal video	yes	personal video	yes
business post	yes	business post	yes	business post	yes
# of views on personal video	100	# of views on personal video	150	# of views on personal video	41
# of engagements on business post	20	# of engagements on business post	10	# of engagements on business post	23

receive? How many engagements did you get on your business post?

There are multiple possible outcomes for your recipe. Let's walk through a few and look at what conclusions we could draw.

Possible Outcome 1

- **Your Ingredients:** Posted twenty personal videos and twenty-one business posts.
- **Your Results:** An average of a hundred and ten views per personal video and twenty engagements per business post.
- **Outcome:** No new business generated.

Since you posted on only twenty of the thirty days, you cannot conclude that the recipe didn't work because you didn't actually follow the recipe exactly, so you need to try again. In the next month, stick to your plan, post every day, and track your results. Based on your results, keep tweaking your recipe until you find a tried-and-true process to get to the desired outcome—one new buyer client.

Possible Outcome 2

- **Your Ingredients:** Posted all thirty personal videos and all thirty business posts.

- **Your Results:** An average of one hundred views per personal video and seventeen engagements per business post.
- **Outcome:** Generated three new potential buyers and signed one client.

Awesome job! You did the work you set out to do and saw the potential, *plus* signed a new buyer! Hello, payday! Now, repeat the recipe. You may want to tweak it a bit to see if you can get better results (e.g., try two personal videos a day instead of one and see if you can generate six leads instead of three).

You now have a recipe that produces a good cake. This is the time to decide if the cake was perfect or *almost* perfect. Are you happy with three leads and one new client, or do you want this lead source to produce more? If you want more, tweak the recipe. If you are happy with it, then bake the cake again exactly the same way.

Possible Outcome 3

- **Your Ingredients:** Posted zero personal videos and zero business posts.
- **Your Results:** No views.
- **Outcome:** No new business generated.

Sometimes (or very often), we have great intentions with not-so-great execution. We have an "A" plan with an "F" or "D" execution. That's *okay*. If you have a bad day, a bad week, or a bad month—and you absolutely will—that does not mean you should pack up and go home. My fitness coach once told me, "Just because we get a flat tire doesn't mean we total the car." Success lies on the other side of failure. So, get back up and try again. As one of our *The Faithful Agent* podcast guests put it, "Don't give up. You don't know if you're on the fifty-yard line or the five-yard line about to score a touchdown."

Success lies on the other side of failure. So, get back up and try again.

In any of the above scenarios, pay careful attention to the outcome. You used your recipe (or didn't) and baked the cake. How did the cake "taste"? Did some of your videos/posts get more views than others? If so, why? What was unique about those? Did certain business posts receive no engagement while others had lots of activity? Why? What was unique about those? Look deeper at the outcome than simply what's on the surface.

Now, if you did not actually post anything at all, of course it did not work. You cannot *sit* your way to success; you *act* your way to success. If you ran your recipe or a partial recipe, then run it again for thirty days, doing more of the videos people liked in the first thirty days. Do it over and over until you have a tried-and-true recipe. It's not hard; it just requires consistency and a willingness to try. You cannot control the results, but you can control the work. Your job is input, not output. Put in the work, and you will see the results.

Here are the two main data points you want to know:

1. How many personal and business posts does it take to get "x" number of leads/clients?
2. What particular personal and business posts performed better?

You make a recipe, bake the cake, taste the results, and then tweak it and bake it again.

I once had a call from an agent who had purchased my Monthly Touch Plan, which provided the exact lead generation I personally use each month in my own Perfect 36 Touch System (how I generate referrals—more on that later). It was the "easy button" of relational lead generation and had proven to be effective for the many, many agents implementing it.

This agent was calling me to cancel, so I asked her why. She said bluntly, "It doesn't work." Wanting to understand how I could help or improve the system, I dug a little deeper. "I'm sorry to hear that and want to learn more. How consistent have you been in getting the materials out and making the personal touches in the plan?" Her response was, "Very inconsistent. I have not done most of the touches." I responded simply, "Then how do you know the system doesn't work if you haven't worked it?"

In lead generation and in life, often we are too quick to find a scapegoat for our lack of success.

- "This system didn't work because it wasn't good."
- "Why doesn't anyone like my videos?"
- "Instagram reels just don't work."
- "I can't get more business because I didn't grow up here."

Stop making excuses and start taking action. The only way to overcome your own objections is to act your way through it. Messy, confusing, difficult action is *the* pathway to success. Just because there is no physical, tangible result does not mean there was no progress. Even a terrible recipe will still give you a cake.

I'm convinced there are only three traits required to succeed in business:

1. The willingness to try
2. The willingness to fail
3. The willingness to persevere

One of my favorite quotes of all time comes from Charles Kettering, who said, "The only time you can't afford to fail is the last time you try." Put another way: If you refuse to give up, then you'll have a long runway to get your plane off the ground. Not everyone will have a successful takeoff in their first three months. I didn't. Some of us will take longer—as you might recall, it took me five and a half months—before our plane leaves the ground. Some of us will even take off quickly but then need to land the plane due to maintenance problems, and the next takeoff will be more difficult than the first. But if we give ourselves only three months of runway, we will crash. Keep trying. *The continued willingness to try over and over again gives you an infinite runway to success.*

    There is no shortcut to this process. Even following someone else's system *does not mean* it will work the exact same way for you. There are thousands of variables. I am not a young, attractive agent. I'm a middle-aged dude who loves to eat. I'm probably not going to have as many followers as a young and attractive female agent will, and therefore, I may not be as effective on social. But even if you're like me, you've got to decide on a recipe, follow it exactly, bake the cake, and continue tweaking the social media recipe until the perfect cake comes out. Then, and only then, will you know your exact recipe for your exact taste buds.

Once you know the predictable result from your purposeful actions, you can build a very easy business plan. For example, you may discover that by posting one video every day with your kids for three hundred and sixty-five days, you can generate forty-eight leads and twenty-four closings. Yes, it's that simple. And remember, once you find the right recipe, your business will only continue to improve as you gather more likes and followers. So eventually, the same work—one video a day with your kids—could go from twenty-four closed deals to thirty-six closed deals in a year. Pretty sweet.

A friend of mine who's a brilliant social media marketer said, "It's called a social media *feed*. Social media is your baby. If you haven't fed your baby in five days, you're a bad parent." Feed that baby and bake that cake.

Recipe #2: Referrals

Hypothetically, let's imagine you run across someone who has a phenomenal 36 Touch campaign. It's tried-and-true, simple to execute, and the end result is tons of business. (I have one just like that. Go to thebalancedbreakthrough.com/course and I'll show you the exact model.) So, you get the course and you want to test it out.

Now, let me pause and explain what a "36 Touch" system is in case you are unfamiliar with the term. A 36 Touch system is designed to generate repeat and referral clients from the people you already know. It's built on a standard of connecting with your sphere of influence (often considered your database) thirty-six times per year through mail, email, and personal reach-outs.

As I said above with social media, just because my recipe is tried-and-true and has produced at least fifty closed deals a year, seven years in a row for me, does not mean you will have the exact same result. This is my recipe; it works for my taste buds. Yours might taste different.

So, how do you test the recipe and track its result? Just like you tested social media. Either run my Perfect 36 Touch playbook (or someone else's) or create your own. Yours could have fifty touches or one hundred touches or however many you want to test. As long as you create a recipe that you will actually execute on, it doesn't matter how many touches are involved.

For example, perhaps you want to try my Perfect 36 Touch campaign to your database.

36 Touch Recipe:

- Monthly Mailer
- Monthly Email
- Quarterly Client Event

- Quarterly Phone Call
- Quarterly Handwritten Note

Understand the recipe, then, do it. Bake that cake, girl (or guy—it just didn't sound as good like that). Keep track of everything you do (go to thebalancedbreakthrough.com/track to get your own tracker): who you wrote notes to and when, who you texted, who you called, who you dropped a pop-by gift to, and so on . . . and then measure the results.*

Remember that a referral is always a lagging indicator of the relationships you are building. That is, you may not get a referral right away, but you are making emotional deposits into your clients' lives and hearts and creating more opportunity for them to refer you. Your job with a 36 Touch program is to execute the *right touches consistently* to *the right people* (your database). In chapter 10 I'll show you my personal PDA Formula, which is my Perfect 36 Touch system.

---

* In relational marketing like this, it is a little more difficult to see direct correlation between one act of reaching out to your database and receiving a referral—just like you will not always know exactly which social post generated business. I get asked all the time if pop-bys or client events yield the most referrals, and my answer is always the same: I don't know. It is a culmination of my consistent effort to love on and care for my people that generates referrals. It's the magic of PDA (not the high school lovey-dovey version).

For example, let's say that for ninety days, you follow my Perfect 36 Touch. You send a postcard to your entire database of one hundred people, then an email, followed by a video text, a handwritten note, and a client event. At the end of ninety days, you have touched your database nine times (three postcards, three emails, three personal touches).

Possible Outcome 1: You nailed it! You had 100 percent execution, and you generated four new potential buyers and sellers. So, you decide to run the same playbook again. The next month, you generate five new buyers and sellers. You run this playbook for a full year and generate twenty-two closed referrals.

The next year, your goal is thirty closed referrals. Since you had such a great response with client events, you decide to host an event every other month for a total of six events a year instead of just four, hoping it increases your closed deals to thirty. If it does, awesome! You have found your recipe. If it doesn't, that's okay! Go back to four events a year and try writing more notes to see if that gets you to your goal. Again, this is a tweaking and retweaking of a recipe until it's perfect, and that takes trial and error. Remember, this takes time. Grandma didn't perfect her secret pound cake recipe in a day.

Possible Outcome 2: You sent your mailers and emails but did not do the personal touches—video text, note, client event. You generated one new client only. That's okay! You still made progress. Run the system perfectly the next three months and watch your results. Tweak as necessary.

Possible Outcome 3: You did nothing and were frustrated with yourself and the outcome. As I tell my kids all the time, "We are allowed to be frustrated if we are willing to do something to change it. We are not allowed to be frustrated if we are unwilling to work to change." For most agents, this is where the rubber meets the road. Are you willing to get back on the horse and go again, or are you content to accept a life of mediocrity far below your God-given potential?

I have never seen a fully executed, well-designed 36 Touch program produce anything other than a positive effect and real business. People in your life want you to succeed. It's your job to show them how they can help. You show them through your consistency of contact and care.

Imagine a 36 Touch system that takes only two hours a week to execute and produces more than fifty closings a year, working only with people you know, like, and trust and who know, like, and trust you too.

It's pretty sweet. That's my business. You can do it too. Bake that cake.

Recipe #3: Prospecting

Let me start by saying that I'm no prospecting master. I've never personally prospected. Based on my observations and conversations with more seasoned and skilled prospectors, here is an example of how I would make my recipe.

Prospecting Recipe

- Make two hours of calls per day, Monday–Friday
- Call between 8:00 and 9:00 a.m. and from 5:00 to 6:00 p.m.
- Call expired listings in the morning
- Call FSBOs (for sale by owners) in the evening

I would try this recipe consistently for a full thirty days, tracking how many actual conversations I had, how many turned into appointments, and how many turned into clients. I would follow one dynamic script for the full thirty days so I could begin to internalize it and then personalize it. I would use a dialer, like Mojo or Vulcan7 to get through as many calls as I could, and I would approach the conversations relationally as opposed to transactionally. That way, I could try and build my database at the same time.

For example, here is the script I would personally use on an FSBO:

> *Hi, Mr. Smith? This is Garrett Maroon with eXp Realty. I saw your home on Main Street is for sale. Have you had any luck finding a buyer?*
>
> *[Possible response: No, not yet.]*
>
> *I'm sorry to hear that. I respect your goal of selling your home on your own and saving the commission, and I'm not calling to try and convince you otherwise. I'll be completely transparent with you, one way I build my own business is by creating a win-win with homeowners like yourself, helping you understand and implement the best sales tactics on your own to help you sell more quickly and for more money. That helps you out. Then later, when you meet a friend or coworker who does not want to sell on their own, you might refer them to me as their listing agent, which helps me out. Would you mind if I came by and shared with you my ten tips for selling by owner?*

Using this script, my goal would be to create new relationships with FSBOs who may end up using me if their home doesn't sell and, hopefully, if a friend wants to sell with an agent they would pass my name along. I would approach this as coming alongside them in pursuit of mutual goals instead of trying to change their mind.

Again, I am not an expert in this area, but I could become one if I chose. I use this as an example of how you could craft your own recipe for mastering a lead-gen area that you currently have no experience with. With enough repetition and refinements to the prospecting recipe, anyone could create a delicious and predictable outcome.

It is important to note here that when it comes to creating your lead generation recipe, it's going to take more than just thirty days to gain all the data and understanding you need. This will be a longer period of trial, error, and tweaking until you get the recipe exactly right. It took me three years to get my referral system dialed in, but once I did, it has produced more than fifty deals a year in less than eight hours a *month* of lead generating. Would you work on something for three years if it meant you could sell fifty homes a year for the rest of your life by working only eight hours a month on lead generation?

It's also essential to decide in advance what each mailer will include, what your notes will say, what the events will be, what social posts you will make, who you will prospect, what you will say, and so on. The more you plan in advance, the higher the likelihood you will actually do the work.

PREDICTABILITY

When I was building my referral system, I printed off a blank hard copy of each month's calendar for an entire year. Then, I wrote down what I needed to do for lead generation each day of the year. That was it. I put nothing else on the calendar. This calendar was not for appointments; it was exclusively for my lead-gen tasks that year.

I sat it on my desk, right next to my computer, and the first thing I did when I got to work each morning was to check what lead-gen activities, if any, I was supposed to do that day. If there was an activity listed, I did it first, before checking my email, social media, voicemails, or texts. If the calendar was blank for that day, meaning no lead-gen activity was required, then I jumped into whatever I wanted to do.

(I use blankcalendarpages.com)

You can see I knew how many notes I wanted to write on note days and how many pop-bys (drop-in visits to a client or potential client) I would deliver on pop-by days. And to be clear, you don't have to schedule a lead-gen activity for every day. Three or four days a week is plenty, and you may even take whole weeks off a few times a year just to prevent the activities from becoming a chore. As you'll see in my example calendar above, I did lead generation tasks only twelve days that month, which means I had eighteen days off. You get lots of rest if you're willing to intentionally run on the right days.

Lead generation is not rocket science. If I was able to figure it out, you shouldn't have any trouble. Lead generation simply boils down to an effective system (our recipe) that you work consistently and that creates a predictable outcome.

Now, you may be thinking, *I hate systems, I'm just a people person. Systems will cramp my style.* Well, maybe your style needs some cramping! That might just be an excuse getting in the way of your goals. I call my form of relational lead generation *systematic relationships*. No, those words don't contradict. Think of it like this: The most important relationships in my life are my wife and my kids. Once a month, Rachel and I have a Wednesday date night. Every other week, we have a daytime date on Wednesdays from 10:30 a.m. to 1:00

p.m. Every Friday night is family fun night. I schedule repeated, consistent time with the people I love and care about most. Why? Because they are a priority, and I need to make sure I show up consistently. It's a system that ensures I show them how much I care.

Date night is a system. Family pizza and movie night is a system. The truth is, you can turn anything in your life that you truly care about into a system. Maybe you go fishing every week. System. Maybe you travel out of the country twice a year. System. Maybe you go to the gym every morning. System.

Creating your lead-gen recipe and following it over and over is not restrictive; it's freeing. You know that you have prioritized what needs to be a priority. You now know the exact work needed to produce an exact amount of closed business. Nothing is more freeing than that. And remember, just like baking a cake, it takes time to gather the ingredients, time to mix the ingredients, time to season the ingredients, and time to bake. It takes *time*. The same is true for our lead generation efforts, so be patient.

As we wrap up this chapter, I want to add one more principle for you to consider as you create your own recipes. That principle is *simplicity*. Most of the time, we think in terms of *possibility* when we really need to think in terms of *probability*. What do I mean? When we design our lead generation recipes, it's common to create a very comprehensive, really intricate strategy we think would absolutely dominate. It requires five activities a day, five days a week, fifty-one weeks a year, or some similarly absurd structure that we decide in January is a good idea but in truth will happen only if literally everything in our life goes perfectly . . . and it never does.

In our minds, anything is possible, right? And it is. It's possible I could dunk a basketball. It's possible I could become the next US president. It's possible I could sell five hundred houses all by myself in one year. Most everything is possible. But that's not the correct mindset. Instead, we need to think, *Is this probable?* What's the probability of me dunking a basketball? About 5 percent. (Okay, -5 percent.) How probable is it that I could sell five hundred homes in a year if I lead generate for ten hours a day? One percent.

After you design your lead generation recipe, I want you to look at it and ask yourself, *What's the probability I will execute all of this consistently for three months?* If the answer is not 90 percent or higher, then your recipe is too complex, and you need to cut something out. Simplify it until you arrive at a 90 percent or higher probability of execution. Simplicity, scale, and consistency will always beat creativity. You want to build the simplest lead generation strategy to accomplish your sales goals.

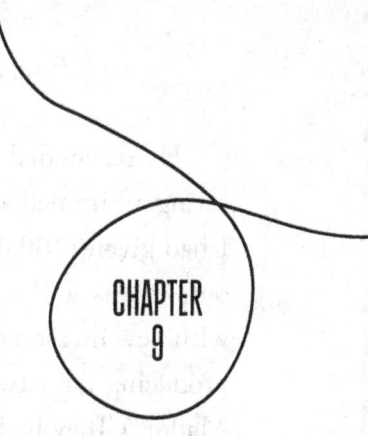

Chapter 9

Profitability

"Brother, please tell me you did not make that investment."

I woke up at 5:30 a.m. to that text from my closest friend, Tyler, on a Wednesday in the middle of May.

I had spent the better part of a year devouring books on investing and tax strategy, finally taking seriously my responsibility to be a good steward of my financial resources.

"What investment?" I asked.

"The CO_2 Scrubbers."

"Yes, I put in $100,000." I had spent a month researching this company, talking to multiple people I knew who had invested already, learning about the technology, understanding its impact in the oil and gas fields . . . but nothing is foolproof.

He responded with a link to an SEC report indicating an immediate court order against the company I had given $100,000 only two months earlier. Turns out, it was a Ponzi scheme. (Paying early investors with new investors' money to create the appearance of producing an actual profit and return—think Bernie Madoff.) They had collected over $155 million in five years. At that moment, I knew I'd likely never see that $100,000 again.

That's what I call the complete opposite of being dollar-productive. I was dollar *unproductive* with that hundred grand. Giving someone a pile of cash and getting a return of $0 was not my finest moment. It still stings.

Productivity and Perspective

I want to take a quick diversion for just a minute before we dive too deep into dollar productivity. There's an important lesson we've got to learn if we ever hope to fully embrace the concept of dollar productivity, and that lesson is about *perspective*.

Back in 2012, Rachel and I had been married for only two months. We were in our new home getting ready for our first Christmas together as husband and wife. I woke up on the morning of December 19 and came slowly down the steps to make coffee as I always did.

PROFITABILITY

As I descended into the living room, I noticed that our couch cushions were lying randomly around the room. Still partially asleep, I kept coming down the steps, confused as to why the couch was that way. As I scanned the rest of the room, my eyes moved from our couch to the door to the two living room windows—which were both wide open—to our mantle and our Christmas tree. Then, I started to understand what was going on. Our TV was gone. All our Christmas presents . . . gone. Still in denial, I walked over to the open windows that overlooked our driveway. That's when it really hit me. Both cars were gone. We'd been robbed in the middle of the night.

I ran upstairs to tell my wife, who was in the shower. She said my face looked pale. I could barely comprehend what had happened when I called the police to report it. Our cars were gone. Our wallets were gone. Our keys were gone. We had no form of ID, no credit cards, nothing. (We later realized they had come up the stairs, past our bedroom while we slept, and stolen our lockbox, which contained our passports, Social Security cards, and birth certificates.) It was a terrifying and violating feeling.

About two hours later, my parents arrived to help. Later that morning, my mom drove us to a car rental lot. I rode in front next to Mom, and Rachel sat in the back seat. My mother, sensing our anxiety and sense of loss, looked at me and said, "Just remember, honey, everything truly important is still in the back seat."

My wife was safe. *We* were safe. They had just taken stuff, and stuff could be replaced. We got the car and came home to a crazy day trying to navigate bank accounts, stolen Social Security cards, credit cards, and car insurance. Wild.

Since you're probably curious, I'll tell you that they never found who did it. They most likely broke in through the windows and took whatever they could.

However, a few days after the robbery, I got a call from my college-roommate-turned-narcotics-officer. "Garrett, did you guys have a car stolen? I think I just found it." He had personally pulled up behind four teenagers suspected of doing drugs. When he turned on his sirens they jumped out of the car while it was still moving and took off. In an insane coincidence, that was Rachel's car. My car was found a week later sitting on the side of the road in a random neighborhood. A neighbor called it in and said they had never seen a car like that in their neighborhood and assumed it was stolen. They were right. We got it back.

It never felt quite right to sit on that couch or drive in those cars knowing someone else had been there without our permission. It's a strange and violating feeling.

What does this have to do with being dollar-productive? For me, it's a reminder to be purposeful in willfully choosing to have the right perspective in difficult moments. You often can't change your reality, but you can change your perspective. Rachel and I have been robbed at home, I've been robbed as a teller when I worked at a bank right out of college (that's another story for another time), and I've had $100,000 stolen in a Ponzi scheme. And yeah, that all stinks.

You often can't change your reality, but you can change your perspective.

But as my mom reminded me, stuff is just stuff. Stuff is not satisfaction or joy. There's a reason the Bible tell us in Matthew 6:19–20 (ESV), "Do not lay up for yourselves treasures on earth, where moth and rust destroy and where thieves break in and steal, but lay up for yourselves treasures in heaven, where neither moth nor rust destroys and where thieves do not break in and steal."

When we take a hit, we have to pause and regain perspective. It's been more than ten years since we were robbed, and now, it's just a story we tell. We've sold that house, sold those cars, and moved on. You can take hits and keep going. They hurt much less with the proper perspective. I've also lost my mom, and Rachel has lost her dad. We would gladly give up $100,000 to spend more time with either of them, and we'd consider it a blessing to write that check. That's a far cry from how I felt realizing I'd flushed a hundred grand down the toilet with that crummy investment.

Perspective gives clarity. Perspective gives us the proper response to life events.

What Is Dollar Productivity?

What do I mean by "dollar-productive"? Simply put, it's intentionally investing as little money as possible to get the greatest return possible.

"Duh, Garrett, we all do that."

But do you? Do you *really*?

It's far too common to meet agents who purchased a "lead-gen system" for $1,000 a month and signed a contract for a full year but no longer work the "leads" and still have seven months remaining on that commitment. It's too common to meet agents who were convinced Zillow leads were their ticket to happiness and instead of investing $500 for three months to test the waters, they dove into the deep end, dropped $3,000 a month, and ended up barely getting a return—or at least, not as strong of one as they could have. If you have not done this, you know someone who has.

Instead, this is what it looks like to be dollar-productive: Start with a small financial investment and squeeze and squeeze and squeeze until you have gotten every possible dollar out of it. Then, and only then, invest more money.

Say you invested $1 and got a $5 return. Before you spend another dollar, ask yourself, *How can I get that same $1 to return $7 instead?*

Here's a real-life example: As I was building my Perfect 36 Touch system, I started with fancier, more expensive client events that featured bounce houses, live music, caterers, ice cream trucks, and so on. They cost me, on average, around $2,500 per event, and I was doing four events a year. Including that $10,000, I was spending around $25,000 total every year on my touch system—mailers, pop-by gifts, client events, client lunches, and so on. The return on that $25,000 was around $300,000 in GCI (gross commission income). So, every $1 I spent returned $12. Not bad. Not bad at all.

But then, I asked myself, *How can I get that same $1 to return $30 instead?* I aimed to do this by both cutting costs and increasing revenue. I kept executing the same system but gradually reduced the size and scope of my client events and pop-by gifts. The client event cost went from an average of $2,500 to only $800. My pop-by gift average went from $750 a year to $200 a year, and so on. I kept trimming the fat on expenses and was intentional with where I needed to spend money—and where I *didn't* need to.

So, how did I do in my attempts to squeeze $30 out of $1? In 2022, I spent only $10,000 for the whole year on my system and generated almost $900,000 in GCI. A whopping $90 return on every $1 put in! The more I asked that question—*How can I get this same $1 to return "x" instead?*—the more my brain worked to solve that problem.

Let's back up a minute. Most of us would be more than happy with a $12 return on a $1 investment, and I was. There was one difference, though. Most agents would then take that system and simply spend more money doing the exact same thing, constantly getting a $12 return on every dollar spent. And truthfully, that would be a really good business. But to achieve a $900,000 GCI in that model, it would cost $75,000. That's still a good business, but it's not the best *possible* business.

If I offered you a business that cost you $75,000 and generated $900,000 or a business that cost you $10,000 and generated $900,000, which would you take? You're probably thinking, *I would take either one.* You're not wrong, but which is the *best* business?

Instead of being satisfied with my $12 return, I kept squeezing and squeezing that dollar until I maximized the amount it returned to me. (Truthfully, I'm not even sure I've gone as far as I can with it. I still believe I can get closer to $100 out of every $1.)

That is what I mean by being dollar-productive.

Here is the typical agent's spending pattern. Let's call this agent Steve. He's two years into the business and does around fifteen deals a year, just enough to be full-time and take care of his family but not enough to shake the burdensome game of "Where's my next commission coming from?"

Steve meets Janet, an agent in his office, who is selling thirty homes a year. Ten of those sales come from online leads, where she is spending $2,500 a month.*

Steve barely has an extra $1,000 to spend on his business, but he wants to sell more homes, and he sees how well online leads are working for Janet. So, Steve does what most agents do: He signs up for the shiny object and invests $1,000 a month, hoping

---

* Note: I am pulling real numbers from agents I know who use online lead platforms. They average a 1 percent conversion rate and a $30/lead spend, which is why ten sales for Janet would cost $2,500/month or $30,000/year. These numbers fluctuate in different markets, and I know there are many different online lead platforms, costs, and so on, but the example still applies no matter the system.

he can get a similar conversion as Janet. Sound like anyone you know?

Let's back up and evaluate this decision. If Steve also has a 1 percent conversion rate and his $1,000 buys him thirty-three leads per month, then that means Steve will close a sale once every three months, or four closings a year.

The median sales price across the country in September 2023 (according to NAR) was $394,300.[7] According to listwithclever.com, the average agent commission per transaction is between 2.77 and 2.67 percent[8] (you may be getting more or less depending on your area). Using 2.67 percent, that means each sale Steve earns (remember, he closes four per year) makes him $10,527 in commission. Four closings per year comes to $42,111 in commissions through online leads.

As agents, despite what the public thinks, we don't keep every dime of that commission. Oh, how I wish it were so. Say Steve works for a broker that has an 80/20 split (I know this varies wildly). Steve pays his office $8,422 and keeps $33,688. Steve then has expenses, dues, and other costs; he typically nets around 80 percent of his portion of the commission since he runs a lean business. That leaves Steve with $26,951 in profit from his online leads. *But wait*, there's more.

Then, the tax man comes a knockin'. According to Robert Kiyosaki in *Rich Dad's Cashflow Quadrant*, the

PROFITABILITY

average self-employed business owner pays an effective tax rate of 40 percent.[9] So, $10,780 of the $26,951 goes to the government, leaving $16,171 in Steve's pocket. Finally.

We get all that, right? That's as close to a real-world scenario as we can imagine. We all live in these kinds of numbers every day. So, let's see how Steve ultimately fared on his investment in online leads.

Steve spent $12,000 to net $16,171, giving him an actual profit of only $4,171, or just over $1,000 per closing. To make that four grand, he had to chase down four hundred "leads," ditch his family in the middle of dinner probably fifty times, and run himself ragged trying to meet that "speed to lead" requirement.

Forget turning $1 into $5 or $7 or $12. Poor Steve was spending $1 to make $1.35. Ouch.

That shiny online lead idea doesn't seem so great anymore, does it? They weren't selling Steve leads; they were selling him a false sense of hope . . . and he bought it.

But let's assume Steve can get his 1.35 to 1 return on online leads up to at least a 2 to 1 return, meaning he profits $2,000 for every $1,000 he spends. Would that mean Steve made a bad decision for his business? Not at all. But did he make the best decision? Also no.

Constantly needing to spend money for poor or low returns is simply chasing your tail. You're in the hamster wheel and will always be in the hamster wheel. See, success is not choosing between bad and good; it's about choosing between good and best.

Success is not choosing between bad and good; it's about choosing between good and best.

Steve had been closing ten deals a year from his sphere of influence and referrals, though he only occasionally sent anything to his database or took anyone to lunch. Those ten deals made him (using the same median sales price and commission) $105,278 in GCI and $40,426 in net profit after paying the brokerage, his expenses, and 40 percent in taxes. The good news is that he spent only $3,000 on those relationships for the whole year. The even better news is that 91 percent of people choose a referral over anything else, so instead of needing one hundred online leads to close one house, he needed one referral to close one house. He was getting a $13 return for every $1 he was spending on his database and a *much* better return on his time and sanity. Is that better than online leads? Absolutely.

Okay, that was a lot of math. You might want to take a quick breath and give your brain a break after digesting all that . . .

Now, let's revisit Steve's first meeting with Janet. Janet talked about how great her online leads were, which got Steve interested in investing $1,000 in the hope of selling a few more homes a year. What should Steve's thought process have been?

He could have thought, *I like this idea, but before I do it, I wonder what would happen if I invested that money in a different area. Could I get an even higher return?*

Better yet, he might have considered, *Could I spend less than $1,000 and make more than $2,000?*

I wish I had done this before I "invested" $100,000 into a Ponzi scheme. I learned the hard way what happens when you skip this question. I could have invested that same money into my business that I control, won't steal from, and likely had a much better return than the Ponzi scheme promoted.

You see, we often do not truly hold our dollars accountable for working as hard as they possibly can. We tend to overspend to avoid the tougher and deeper work. If we just throw money at the problem, we don't have to keep leveling up in our chosen area of lead generation to make our dollars stretch further and further. My Ponzi scheme investment was the "easy" way. We can simply keep spending and only ever achieve mediocrity in return.

Harsh? Sure. But it's also true.

Think about the last time you spent money on your business. Did you look at every way you were generating new clients, determine your dollar return, and then strategically invest your money into what you believed would give you the absolute best return on each dollar? Or did you run your business on hope and shiny objects, like Steve, following the crowd into the next best thing?

It constantly blows my mind how much money agents spend on the *good* but not the *best*. According to the National Association of Realtors, 91 percent of clients would choose a referral over anything else—91 percent.[10] And yet how many millions (maybe billions) of dollars do agents spend each year chasing that other 9 percent? And how many millions do they spend trying to connect with the 91 percent? I'm not aware of any statistical data on this, but my experience tells me that for every $1 someone spends on their database (the 91 percent), they're spending about $10 on the others (the 9 percent). Talk about being dollar-*un*productive. For some reason, we have become satisfied with a smaller return on our investment, but any smart investor would tell you that's not the game to play.

Why is it so common for agents to spend so much on the good but not the best (or even bad) lead-gen systems? Why do we seem to hit the bulls-eye of mediocrity nine times out of ten?

This is one of the most pervasive issues I see in the real estate world today. It's what drives us to overspend, build our teams too big, speak too big of a game—we're looking at the wrong scoreboard.

We look at the scoreboard around us and have an innate desire to sell as many homes as Agent X in our office because they closed thirty deals and got the gold award, while we only sold twenty homes and got the silver award. What you don't know is, Agent X had a profit of $50,000 only because he spent so much money trying to generate those thirty sales while you had a profit of $85,000 because you were dollar-productive.

Which business would you choose:

- **Business A:** Fifty transactions a year, $500,000 in GCI, top 1 percent in your region, and $100,000 net profit

—OR—

- **Business B:** Thirty transactions a year, $300,000 in GCI, top 10 percent in your region, and $175,000 net profit?

That's a no-brainer, right? (At least I hope it is.) But our actions often say differently, specifically with money. We just want to get to that higher number, higher GCI, higher ranking. We are not focused on squeezing every single dollar out of each dollar we spend.

Why?

Pride. Ego. Vanity.

Sometimes, we simply value the *acclaim* more than the *income*.

Now, I'm not just pointing the finger at you; I'm pointing the finger at myself too. It's difficult to not use that industry scoreboard—which assigns more points to vanity—even if it results in less money and ROI. I've already told you where this all started for me. I had a team with three agents and three admins. Then, I woke up one day and asked myself *why*. I didn't actually want it; I had simply allowed my focus on the industry's scoreboard to dictate my direction and actions. So I wanted more sales, higher GCI, and a better ranking (at least that's what I told myself).

I've heard it said that you have only two accounts: a bank account and an ego account. You can put money into only one of those accounts, so choose wisely.

When you spend money just to generate more sales without a focus on net profit—that feeds your ego account. When you very intentionally try to generate even more sales from your database through personal touches that don't cost you money—that feeds your bank account. When you spend thousands upon thousands of dollars and end up barely profitable but boast about being ranked in the top 1 percent—ego account. When you purposefully go about your work to maximize how much money you actually keep on each transaction, even if it's not flashy or Instagram-worthy—bank account.

I learned this firsthand when one of my buddies, who has a large team of more than fifteen agents and spends over $20,000 a month on buying "leads," showed me his profit and loss statement. His team had sold more than three hundred homes and had a GCI of $2.7 million. He was doing way more volume than my team was. I was impressed . . . until I dug further into the P&L. The numbers didn't lie: He was spending so much money trying to generate leads, paying inside sales agents, paying admin staff, and leasing office space that he actually profited less money than I did with far fewer closings and a team of myself, one other agent, and an admin at that time.

I don't know about you, but I would choose simple and more profitable over complex and less profitable any day of the week. Don't let your ego account steal from your bank account.

That's dollar productivity. You start with, *How can I make this $1 produce more and more dollars?* and then ask, *How can I make this hour worth more and more?*

Let's dig into time productivity by looking at an example of the opposite, more typical real estate agent. In this scenario, you don't have set hours, so you end up working about sixty hours a week. You have "vacation," but let's be honest, that's really just working from somewhere else. So, you end up averaging sixty hours a week for fifty-one weeks, or 3,060 hours of work for the year. If you want to earn $200,000 per year, you have to earn $65.35 per working hour ($200,000 divided by 3,060 hours).

You get different answers when you ask yourself, *How do I make this hour worth $100?* than when you ask, *How do I make this hour worth $65?* It forces you to squeeze more return out of each dollar you spend and maximize your investment.

Most of the challenge lies in our inability and unwillingness to squeeze as much money as possible out of each dollar we spend on our lead generation efforts. Our go-to response is usually something like, *I want to go from $200,000 to $400,000 this year, so I guess I'll need to work twice as many hours.* No, no, no. A much better, more efficient, and potentially sanity- and marriage-saving solution would be to ask, *How do I make this hour and this dollar stretch even further and maximize my return?*

In 2019, each dollar I invested produced $30 of GCI and around $10 of profit. So, to make $200,000 I had to invest $20,000. The *only* way to earn more was to either spend more time working (which I was unwilling to do) or make each dollar more productive.

By 2022, I had tripled my return on each dollar invested, bringing it to $90 GCI, or $30 in profit. So,

I chose to work a third of the time (or twelve hours a week) and still made $200,000 that year just from my real estate sales business. How does that sound?

Now, you don't have to follow my path; you might have chosen to keep working the same amount of time and triple your earnings. I chose to scale back my hours so I could do more of what I wanted—podcasting, writing, coaching, and teaching.

I hope this is starting to make sense. It is really important to squeeze as much as possible out of each dollar and each hour you invest into your work. Use the proper scoreboard, build your life, and then design a business that serves that life. Take your newly created lead-gen recipe and keep tweaking and tweaking until it gives you as much money per dollar and per hour as possible. Then, you will have a dollar-productive business. And more importantly, you will have a life by design.

That said, I must inject a word of caution. It's easy to strive for something, believing that we will eventually be able to sit, take it easy, and enjoy the fruits of our labor. But is that really how it works? If we are honest, at the end of all that striving, we usually just find *more* striving—a new and bigger goal, a desire to see how far we can actually go. This is not inherently bad, but it is dangerous. We can convince ourselves and our loved ones that we are just in a short season of maximum effort to reach a goal and that we will stop once we get there. Sometimes, though, that's just a lie—one we don't even realize is a lie until we have already started a second season of maximum effort. So be careful, be aware, and use the right scoreboard.

How to Maximize Each Dollar

I want to get really practical at the end of this section to build on our predictable lead-gen recipe and the desire to be dollar-productive. So, let's go back to the three examples of recipes we discussed in chapter 8—social media, the Perfect 36 Touch system, and prospecting. How can we intentionally make each system more dollar-productive?

Social Media

One of the best parts of social media is the cost: free. One of the challenges is the significant amount of noise and competition. The first rule of social media dollar productivity is: *Never spend money until you are certain you have maximized your return with free content.* Once they have maximized their results without spending money, many agents want to level up their social media by producing higher-quality videos (a

PROFITABILITY

great idea, by the way). What does it look like to be dollar-productive in this scenario?

First, always ask the question, *How little can I spend to accomplish my goal?* If you take nothing else away from this section, take this point. Ask this question constantly on everything you are doing. Do you need the $1,000 camera, or would a $250 camera work? Do you need the $3,000/month video producer, or would a local university student do it for $500? Until you know—*and I mean truly know*—that the lower-cost option will not produce the desired result, do not spend the extra money.

Being dollar-productive looks like spending $500 a month on video production with the goal of creating two extra closed sales for the year. Then, before you hire the $3,000 video producer, assuming it will create ten closings just because it's more expensive, you should work with the $500 producer to squeeze two or three more closings out of their work.

For example, let's assume you receive an average $10,000 in commission each time you close on a house, and you can generate ten closings with the $3,000/month producer. Those ten closings cost you $36,000 in video production costs and generate $100,000 in GCI—that's a return of $2.77 for every $1 spent.

Not bad.

But also . . . not great.

It's workable as long as you can keep spending that much money and stay on top of the videos. But again, what is the probability you can keep this up over the long run?

But what would happen if you kept squeezing the dollar you're investing with the $500 producer and closed five deals for the year? Your cost for the year would be $6,000 in video production costs, and you'd generate $50,000 in GCI—a much better return of $8.33 for every $1 spent.

(Of course, you can also try to squeeze more out of the $3,000/month producer as well, but that's not the point.)

Both are good businesses, but only one is the best business. Don't let your spending get ahead of you. Spending extra should only be the *second* option after you have maximized the dollar you're *already* spending.

Perfect 36 Touch System

I started my search for dollar productivity backward. I began by spending more money, assuming I needed to in order to produce the desired result. It's a common mistake most of us make. Instead, I should have started spending very little and determined whether that would produce my goal *before* I committed to spending any extra.

When I launched my Perfect 36 Touch system, I started with one of the nicer mailers (big and shiny), expensive pop-by gifts ($10 a person), and fancy client events (averaging $2,500, as I mentioned earlier). I was not running through the proper process of starting with a small spend first, squeezing every dollar out of it before increasing the spend—if that was even necessary.

Now, my system was still very dollar-productive. It was good; it just wasn't the best possible. From 2016 to 2019, I overspent on my system by about $15,000 per year, or $60,000 total for those four years. That's a lot of money—money I could have invested or used to take my wife to Europe . . . or bought the most delicious donut money could buy. Man, I wonder how good a $15,000 donut would taste . . .

Anyway, the point is that I started with the more expensive options when I should have started with the less expensive options. If your current 36 Touch system, or the recipe you create, costs you $4,000 per client event, you should ask yourself how you could throw an event for $2,000 instead. If your mailers cost $200 a month, ask yourself how you could cut that to $100 a month. Then, track the result. If it's not producing the desired result, tweak your recipe first and only then increase your spend *if necessary*.

IMPORTANT! As agents, we tend to misunderstand what value we truly bring to our database and clients. We often think a $10 gift is better than a $2 gift or a $4,000 party is better than a $2,000 party. But what gift do the people in our database truly want more than anything else? A friendship. Connection. Someone who will be present with them. Someone who will care for them consistently. Someone who will always show up.

In 2023, the US surgeon general said we were experiencing an "epidemic of loneliness."[11] An extra $2,000 on a party will never make up for a sincere desire to reach out and care for your people. You could spend the extra two grand, or you could be intentional in building a relationship with them. Being present is free, and the by-product of your presence is more business.

The most dollar-productive activity in your business is simply showing up for someone.

Prospecting

One of the most dangerous lead-gen systems when it comes to dollar productivity is prospecting. We are constantly bombarded with options of spending money on shiny objects that at best produce a 5 percent conversion rate. Don't hear me say there isn't a place for this with some agents, but *do* hear me say: *We often spend money on our intentions instead of our practices.* Let me explain.

Agent Steve (remember him?) knows he needs to do something for his business. His leads aren't where they need to be, and he isn't making enough money. He hears about a great system that costs $500 a month. This system requires two hours a day of cold-calling the leads, which he has never done before, but he's desperate. He has to do *something*.

So, even though he has never made cold calls before, let alone done it for two hours a day, he buys the system, signs a twelve-month contract, and gets to work.

In this example, Steve just purchased a system based on his *intentions* instead of his *practices*. He *hopes* he will create a new habit and routine to make his spend worth it. What's the likeliest outcome? That he won't follow through. There are lots of reasons for this, including misalignment (more to come on that in the next chapter).

When it comes to prospecting (and most anything else), develop your practice first and then spend the money to bolster the practice. Just like social media, you want to create the recipe, make all the posts, taste the cake, and *then* determine if you need to spend money to enhance the work you are *already doing*. Develop the routine first.

Here's how this could look in prospecting: You already have a cell phone, and you can find the phone numbers of FSBOs for free. Start by creating the practice of calling FSBOs for one hour a day. Once you've developed that routine and know you will continue doing it, spend a little money to enhance your work. Just start small.

For example, you might purchase the information of absent owners and work that list using your same old cell phone. The more proficient you become, the more it makes sense to purchase the supporting tools you might need, like an automated dialer. The key is to start with the free, do the work, and track the results. Focus on two data points:

1. Did you generate sales?
2. Did you stay consistent on your prospecting recipe?

If your answers are yes and yes, fantastic! Now, you can find the cheapest possible option to enhance the work you're already doing and bake the cake again (only sweeter).

The problem in prospecting is the same problem we all have when it comes to starting a new routine, like going to the gym. When we make that New Year's resolution to exercise, what do we do? We buy the gym membership, but we don't stop there. We also buy the workout gear, the whey protein, the shaker bottle, the new sneakers . . . and we haven't even been to the gym yet.

I get it. I do it too. But it's a problem. Once you decide to start prospecting, do it first, then get the stuff you need. When you decide to go to the gym, first wear the clothes and shoes that are already in your closet, and then get the fun stuff in late February—after you've proven to yourself that working out has become a practice, not just an intention.

Which Account Will You Feed?

Being dollar-productive is just good business. But since our rational thoughts are not the only things that play a role in our decision-making, we wrestle with feeding our bank account or our ego account. If all you care about is the rankings, then go ahead and spend yourself into a vicious cycle that never ends. Feed your ego account. Go hog wild!

But I caution you: That will never be truly satisfying. If you'd rather feed your bank account, then do this first: Before you can truly focus on the best business and squeeze as much as possible out of every dollar, sit down and get clear on the scoreboard you really want to use. Write out your life by design, build your scoreboard from it, and then decide what kind of business practices will serve that life. If you keep focused on that scoreboard and constantly ask yourself, *How little can I spend to accomplish my goal?*

you will work your way to a highly dollar-productive business.

I know you can do it. I know you can spend less than anyone else in your office and yet land in the top five for GCI. I know you can change the course of your future and generations to come because you focused on maximizing each dollar. I know you can change the community around you with more of your time and money.

Dollar productivity is a call to something greater.

So . . . *carpe diem*—seize the day.

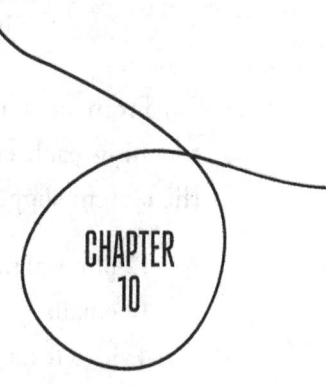

CHAPTER 10

My Personal PDA Formula

Before we wrap this section up, I want you to peek behind the curtain into my own PDA Formula. I've been fortunate (and focused) to build a very predictable and profitable business that aligns with who I am and how I'm wired, and I've shared much of that with you already. Now I'd like to give you the basic framework of my system—the Perfect 36 Touch (just a fancy name for a normal 36-touch system).

If this aligns with you, you can implement a version of it yourself (I also have a much more in-depth e-course on the system you can access at thebalancedbreakthrough.com/course). Perfect 36 Touch is simple, highly effective, and works for everyone who will work it. (I spent three years fine-tuning it.)

From a ten-thousand-foot view, you will be touching each client thirty-six times, as the name of the system suggests:

- **12** physical mailers
- **12** emails
- **4** video texts
- **4** handwritten notes or pop-bys
- **4** client events
- **= 36 "Touches"**

Consistency and care create massive success. It's not one particular touch; it's the combination of your relationship development.

Consistency and care create massive success. It's not one particular touch; it's the combination of your relationship development.

I've done this consistently for nine years, and it typically takes only fifteen hours total for an entire month. The immense growth in your relationships with your database over time, from being intentional month in and month out, will create stability in your business like you've never seen before.

Let me give you some fascinating data. In 1990 Americans were asked how many close friends they have. Twenty-seven percent said fewer than three.[12] Over half said six or more. In 2021, 49 percent said fewer than three and 12 percent even said they have no close friends. If they interviewed them again today, after the entire COVID-19 pandemic era, the rise of social media, increasing political polarization, and other factors, I imagine that number would be closer to 55-60 percent who have fewer than three close friends. We are more connected than ever, but we're also lonelier and more starved for real relationships than ever.

When was the last time someone took the time to write you a personal note, just to let you know they cared about you? When was the last time someone dropped off a gift at your door for no reason other than they cared? When was the last time someone invited you to a fun event just to thank you for being a good friend?

Our real job as real estate agents is being one of those three close friends or taking that to four or five—or, better yet, to ten—because we introduced them to a community. That's what this system does. Plus, people refer people they know to people they like; if you are one of their three close friends, they will think about you. And because they're thinking about you, they will refer you.

So, the Perfect 36 Touch system (my PDA Formula) has a total of thirty-six touches. Obviously, you aren't going to drop thirty-six personal interactions on someone all at once, so what's the right cadence for "dripping" these touches throughout the year?

When I created this system, I wanted to know in advance what kind of lead generation I would hit every month, every week, and every day for the year. Why? Because let's be honest, we never accidentally do what is hard. If you show up to your desk after having a hard client call, your first thought is not, *I want to write some notes!* Instead, it's more likely, *I'm going to waste twenty minutes pretending to be busy by scrolling Facebook or reading emails.*

I've been there many times. That's why I put my lead-gen system on autopilot.

This system allows me to show up, check my calendar, and do what it tells me to do for lead generation. I don't have to think about it, and I don't have to "find time" to do it. I schedule it. It's part of my routine every day/week/month. The result? For the past nine years in a row, I have never missed a month of lead generation. I've done exactly what I intended to do every single month for nearly a decade—and success has followed. Success will follow you, too, when you create your own PDA Formula or follow some version of mine.

MY PERSONAL PDA FORMULA

To help you get going, I've broken the system down into quarters, and each quarter follows the same simple framework:

- **Month 1:** Calls and texts. (Pro tip: If you, like me, don't love talking to people on the phone, send a quick video text. That way, they still see your face and hear your voice without you having to get on the phone with every person every time. An audio-only text is the next best option.)
- **Month 2:** Notes and pop-bys.
- **Month 3:** Events and client coffees.

Along with this, you will send out a physical mailer on the first of each month and an email on the fifteenth of the month.

That's it. There is a simple quarterly flow to it, and then you repeat that same structure for Q2, Q3, and Q4.

Because you will have consistently shown up for your people, they will consistently show up for you. Again, it's the combination of emotional deposits into the life of your people month in and month out. When you are likely one of only three people in their lives consistently checking on them—caring for people at a high level—that itself is success. But the beautiful by-product is repeat and referral business that will lay the foundation for success for years to come.

This is how you future-proof your business against technology, artificial intelligence, or big internet companies, because no one can buy away the relationships that you have and will build with people.

This is how you future-proof your business against technology, artificial intelligence, or big internet companies, because no one can buy away the relationships that you have and will build with people.

Let's see how the PDA Formula works in a real-life workflow:

First Quarter

- January
    - Send a physical mailer on the first and an email on the fifteenth.
    - Send a video text message or regular text, or make a phone call.
- February
    - Send a physical mailer on the first and an email on the fifteenth.
    - Write a note to everyone in your database and deliver a pop-by gift to twenty-five people.

- March
  - Send a physical mailer on the first and an email on the fifteenth.
  - Host a client event.
  - Schedule a coffee date with those who couldn't attend the event to ensure some "face time" with your best contacts and deepen those new or existing relationships.

From there, the cycle repeats beginning in April (Q2), July (Q3), and October (Q4). That's all there is to it. It might feel weird at first, but it gets easier and simpler the more you work the system and actually execute an intentional lead generation plan.

Again, though, this is *my* PDA Formula. You don't have to follow it; in fact, you *shouldn't*—you should create your own. My goal here is to show you what a well-thought-out, scheduled formula looks like and how it empowers you to create a predictable and profitable business that aligns with who you are.

The Two Most Common Questions

Every time I teach this formula to a group or individual, I can expect to hear the same two questions:

1. What do you do for pop-bys, and what kind of gifts are affordable and appropriate?

2. What exactly do you mean by "client events"? That sounds expensive and super complicated.

To save you the trouble of emailing me, let's just tackle those two questions right now.

Pop-By Visits and Gifts

Pop-by visits should be short and sweet. You want them to be warmly received and not seen as intrusive or an inconvenience. In fact, you don't even have to see the person on a pop-by visit! After some trial and error, I figured out what works best for my team's schedule, for our budget, and most importantly, for our clients.

For example, we do two pop-bys to clients who have closed on a house with us. In the days following the closing, we will drop off a gift of a nice gratitude journal. We include a tag on the journal that says:

> In the midst of the busyness of moving, take time to write out what you are most grateful for. A new home, new experiences, new memories. For us, we are most grateful for new friends like you, and we'd love to meet some of your other friends if you know anyone else looking to buy a new home. Enjoy a new month in your new home!

That's a simple and great gift. Just drop it on their door, take a picture, send the picture in a text to the new homeowner, and congratulate them on one month in their new home.

Then, two months after their closing, we drop off a picture frame with a tag that says:

> Take a moment, a breath, to capture the new memories going on in your house. You will never regret stopping to enjoy the normal moments of life. Congratulations on your second month in your new home! If you ever need help with anything or have friends wanting to buy or sell, we would be honored to help them too!

Again, it's short, sweet, and inexpensive, but it is a thoughtful gesture that keeps you top of mind for the new homeowner.

Client Events

The first rule of client events is that they do not need to be expensive or complicated. You aren't planning a wedding or a high school reunion!

One of our most popular events is also one of the simplest. We have coffee and donuts, and I hire a photographer so everybody can come, enjoy some food, and get a free family portrait. We host the event at a local park with animals, and everyone loves it. People have been coming for years, and this is often the only family photo shoot they have for the year. That makes it incredibly meaningful for these families.

Make It Meaningful, Not Transactional

With all of these thirty-six touches, be careful to keep your eye on the prize. Yes, you're doing this to benefit and grow your business, but the most important thing is that you are serving your people at a deep, authentic level. The purpose of the call and text is just to check on them. The purpose of the note and pop-by is to care for them. The purpose of the events and coffee is to celebrate them. That's the whole point: to be a friend—a *real* friend—and not just a real estate agent.

I want to tell you about a client-turned-friend named Nick. This brief story reminds us of the power of a well-executed PDA Formula that aligns with who we are.

Nick was my first client ever, in 2014, and since then, we've developed a friendship.

I remember one day dropping off a pop-by gift at his house. It was a book that was special to me, and I wanted to give him a copy. He wasn't home when I swung by, but his wife and kids were there. His wife opened the door, and I told her I had a present for Nick because I knew his birthday was coming up.

MY PERSONAL PDA FORMULA

She looked at me and said, "Garrett, I don't think you know this, but Nick is not the kind of guy who has a lot of friends. He has some buddies coming in this weekend from Connecticut to see him for his birthday, but . . ." She paused before continuing. "You know, Garrett, truthfully, I think you're his only friend in Virginia."

That story still strikes me to this day because I genuinely love this guy. I want to take care of him and his family and serve them in any way I can. It's not just because he served our country in the military, and it's definitely not because he used me to buy a house. It's because we've developed a real relationship that has come from working my own PDA Formula. I remember leaving his house that day and thinking how honored and humbled I was by what his wife said.

Nick has since sent me literally millions of dollars in business, and that didn't happen by accident. It happened because I had a system (my own PDA Formula) that nurtured our relationship from prospect to client and ultimately to friend.

It took me three years to get the system right, and it will take you time as well, but it's worth it. Build your PDA Formula. Test it. Tweak it. Perfect it. Then enjoy the predictable, profitable, and way-more-enjoyable business you've always desired!

part 4
Intentional Achievement

One of the pivotal moments in my career was in 2018 in a coffee shop with one of my mentors and friends Keith Hinton. It was another gorgeous Virginia summer day. The sun was shining, there was ice cream aplenty (I've always wanted to write that word in a book, and boy does it feel good), and kids were loving the pool.

I was crushing it, too, just like the Virginia weather. I had sold fifty homes a year for the past two years while working less than forty hours a week. I had done it all by relationship and referral. My net profit was over $200,000 per year, and life was pretty good—on the outside.

But inside? Inside, I was a mess.

That morning, I arrived late to our meeting, ordered a coffee, and walked over to where Keith had been sitting for a few minutes already.

I looked him square in the eyes and said, "Keith, I'm ready to quit."

"Good, me too," he responded.

It was his simple, three-word response that changed everything for me. *Wait a minute*, I thought, *Keith owns multiple businesses, makes over $500,000 a year, plays golf almost every day, and yet he wants to quit too?*

That didn't make sense to me. Both of us were succeeding at a pretty high level, making a good living with lots of flexibility, but we both wanted to quit?

What's the point of sharing that story? So you know that I get it. I've been there, and I'm still there. This is hard. Not every day is rainbows and butterflies; sometimes it's thunderstorms and bee stings. I'm not talking about a cute little bumble bee either. I'm talking about one of those kamikazes that feels like it's specifically coming after you, and you don't know why.

It's okay. We are in this together.

Creating a Scoreboard and building your own PDA Formula is incredible, but if we do not purposefully head in our intended direction, then it's only a dream. Dreams without actions are just pain pills: You feel better for a few hours, but then it wears off.

These final few chapters are about making an intentional choice to achieve your scoreboard. Fair warning: It's going to be hard, and there will be lots of bumps in the road, but if you keep moving, you will most certainly fail your way forward. I have yet to meet someone who gave themselves enough of a runway that didn't eventually take off and fly.

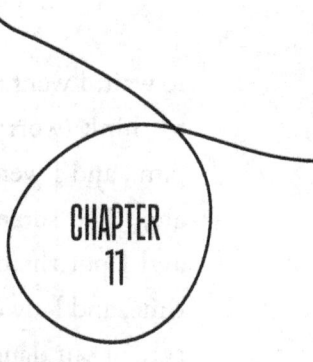

CHAPTER 11

Hierarchy of Attention

It was around 10:00 a.m. on a Wednesday morning when I got a text from my wife that said, "Hey, I added a meeting for us to your calendar for 7:00 p.m. tonight."

That wasn't normal, and I was terrified. No guy likes to hear the love of his life say, "We need to talk," no matter how she phrases it. And we definitely don't want to hear, "We need to talk . . . in nine hours."

"Okay," my trembling thumbs tapped out. "Is everything okay?"

"Yeah, I just wanted to make sure we had time to talk."

I don't know about you, but it's not common for my wife to add appointments to my calendar—especially appointments with her. But what could I do? I just had to wait. I went on with my day, trying (and failing) not to think (worry) about it. Finally, the clock hit 5:00 p.m., and I went home to make the kids' dinner. They ate, I had some good "Daddy time," and then Rachel and I put them to bed. We had only two kids at the time, and I always tucked our son in while Rachel took care of our daughter.

I finished getting Dylan to bed first, so I came downstairs and started making dinner for Rachel and me. It was a few minutes past seven—time for our meeting—but Rachel hadn't made it back downstairs yet. A buddy texted me and asked if I was free to talk. I was in our kitchen alone, so I picked up the phone and called him.

When she came downstairs around 7:10 p.m., I was still on the phone and making dinner. A few minutes later, I wrapped up the call, brought dinner to the table, prayed, and said, "Okay . . . what did you want to talk about?"

My wife looked at me and lovingly said, "*This* is exactly what I wanted to talk to you about. Was that call really important?"

"No."

"Was that call really urgent?"

"No."

"Then why did you take the call when we were supposed to have our meeting?"

She was right.

Granted, I had innocently called my friend while Rachel was still upstairs, so you might think I could cut myself some slack, maybe even get defensive. But I saw that my mindset in that moment was part of a pattern of misaligned priorities that had built up over time. I should have put her and our meeting first.

I immediately thought of a story Brian Buffini (a world-class real estate trainer) shared from early in his career. He also had two kids at the time, and he was on the phone as he walked through the door one evening. His young sons ran up to him, grabbed onto his legs, and excitedly yelled, "Daddy!"

His wife, trying to help him, said, "Boys, don't bother your father. He's not home yet."

That story hit me deeply when I first heard it. Honestly, it still does.

Can we be present without being present? You bet we can. Can we be physically in a room without being mentally or emotionally in a room? All the time. This isn't something we should be proud of; it's something we must actively fight against. I've heard too many stories of top agents who won all the awards, made all the money, and had the biggest teams . . . yet lost their marriages. I've met too many agents who made it to the top but realized when they got there that they'd left all their loved ones behind. Friend, that is just not worth it. If your ambition at work keeps you from being ambitious at home, you've got the order wrong.

We tend to believe we can give all our attention to everyone all the time, but that's impossible. We aren't robots or superhumans; we are people who can be in only one place at a time. That's not how our industry is set up, is it? We work in a business that is obsessed with "always being available," and that's great for the client—but it is awful for you. And it is downright terrible for the people you love the most.

We tend to believe we can give all our attention to everyone all the time, but that's impossible.

Knowing we can focus on only one thing, or on one person, at a time, we've got to start making some hard decisions about who gets our attention and when. That brings us to the *hierarchy of attention*. We've all seen an organizational chart with someone at the top, someone under them, and so on, but you may have never seen an organizational chart for your attention. This is a simple yet incredibly helpful way to keep the main things the main things.

HIERARCHY OF ATTENTION

Here's my hierarchy:

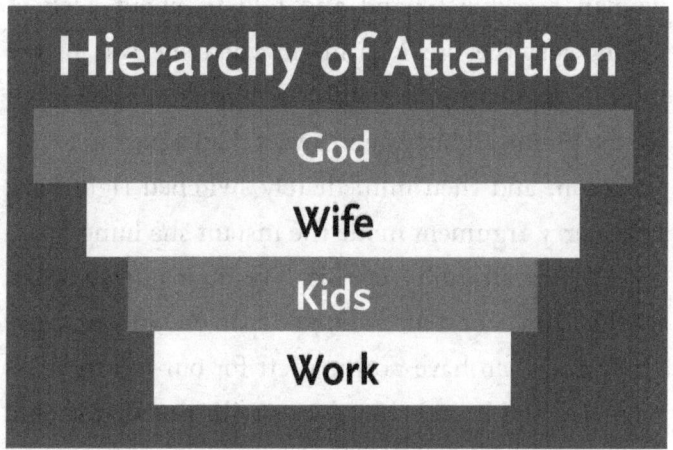

This is a simple snapshot of where I want my attention to go. Of course, I recognize that I'm going to spend far more hours at work than I am with my kids most days. I see my kids for around four hours a day, so they won't get as much attention as my work does. But—and it's a big *but*—the point of this hierarchy is to give us a clear snapshot of the most important relationships in our lives so we can quickly assess how we're doing.

I am guilty of pouring out energy all day at work and then coming home and crashing on the couch with nothing left for my family. I'm even guilty of crashing on the couch but hopping up and putting on a happy, energetic face if a client calls. Weird that I could do it for clients but not for my wife and children, huh?

I was sharing this concept in a seminar when a woman raised her hand and told us about a client calling just the previous night when she was in the middle of an argument with her husband. She picked up the phone all happy and sweet, had a pleasant conversation, and then immediately switched right back into angry argument mode the instant she hung up.

We are all guilty of this. We pour ourselves out to the third- or fourth-ranked person on our hierarchy and then have nothing left for our top three. It happens, and it probably always will. But that should not stop us from fighting in those moments to get our hierarchy back in line—and fighting to devote our time and attention to those who deserve it most.

Have you ever stopped to ask yourself, *Why did I get into this business?* or *Why am I still in this business?*

Many people, myself included, would say, "I got into real estate to better provide for my family and to have more time freedom." That's a great sentiment, but there's a problem. My family was my highest mission, and yet who was getting the least amount of attention? My family. Even worse, I was neglecting my family in the name of "doing this for my family." Talk about misaligned . . .

Nearly every agent I've ever met or taught will say their family is one of the reasons they got into the industry, if not *the* reason. When pressed, though, most of them admit their families have actually suffered in some ways because they got into the business.

How is it that our *good intentions* cause *negative consequences*? My intention is to better serve my family. The unintended negative consequence of that has been countless hours pulled away from them (even when we're in the same room). That's not want I wanted, and if you care so much about your life and loved ones that you're still reading this book, I know that's not what you want either.

The solution to constantly creating unintended negative consequences in your most important relationships is to build out your hierarchy. Think about it like budgeting: If you had one hundred pieces of attention to give (again, we're focused on *attention*, not *time* right now), who or what should get the most pieces? Who holds the preeminent place in your heart? That's your number one. That's the top of your hierarchy.

Then, who should get the second-most pieces? That's the second level of your hierarchy.

Keep going to figure out the third and fourth levels. Then, if there are any pieces left, keep naming people and keep putting them in the hierarchy. But do not try to put *everyone* and *everything* in your hierarchy. If you have one hundred pieces of attention, you can't give one piece to one hundred people. Should your spouse get the same share as your dry cleaner?

Of course not. Besides, your attention is finite. You cannot give all your attention to everything all at once. It's impossible, no matter how often you tell yourself that you're capable of "doing it all."

News flash: You're not. So stop lying to yourself and start telling yourself the truth: *I can be excellent in only a few areas—but I get to choose what those areas are.*

To illustrate the point, write out a list of everything you have to give attention to right now at this moment.

Yeah, it's a lot. Even if you didn't write out the list you know in your mind how large that list is. Mine too. Sometimes we can't get our arms around everything we're trying to do unless we actually write it down and accept how ludicrous it is for us to try to do so much.

With your list in hand, or in your head, look at each item one at a time and ask the hard question: *Is this something I should be spending my precious attention on, or should I let it go? Or at least scale it back?*

My best buddy, Tyler Wilson, gives a great analogy. He is adamant about making our *yes* be yes and *no* be no. He describes it as a firepit burning hot. When we say yes to things, we put rocks in the firepit. All of us have then regretted putting those rocks in the firepit and wish we could cool down that commitment. But most of us leave those rocks in there and accept a continual feeling of burnout, defeat, exhaustion, and frustration, just because we are afraid of the short-term singe of reaching our hands in and pulling the rocks out.

Guess what? It's time to grab some of those rocks out of the fire! Yeah, it may sting, but just think how good it'll feel when they're gone, when several of the things you shouldn't have said yes to in the first place are finally off your plate, lowering the heat and freeing up attention and energy for the people you've put at the top of your hierarchy.

Now let's make it even more practical. It's time to do some spring cleaning on your goals. What on your list did you say yes to that you should have said no to? The top of your hierarchy is wishing you would release the bottom items so you could give more attention to your priorities.

A few nights ago, my wife got the following text from a friend: "Hey, can I come over in the morning and work out with you?"

Nine times out of ten, that would be an instant yes for Rachel. But this time, it wasn't. She told me she didn't really feel up for it because she was so tired from a very busy week, and she knew her friend would want to stick around and hang out afterward. Normally, she would love that, but she didn't think she had the energy for it this time.

Then, she said something we've all felt and used to make decisions a million times: "But she asked, so how can I say no?"

One of the numerous reasons I appreciate my wife is that she often says what we are all thinking. In this case, she felt handcuffed to a yes response simply because the question was asked. Have you ever felt that way? I certainly have. It's a mixture of a fear of missing out, a fear of letting others down, and having no criteria to run our decisions past.

I'll tell you what I reminded Rachel: We always have a choice. Life can't be based on who asks us to do something. The same goes for you: Life must be based on your intentional choice to focus on what you and you alone deem important.

So, she told her friend no, simply saying she was just too tired. Guess what? Her friend was absolutely okay with it. No hurt feelings. No ruined friendship. She said no, and the world didn't end.

It was a great reminder that we can *and should* say no more often and yes more intentionally.

Your life right now might be full of yeses that should have been nos. It might be full of people-pleasing when in reality, the only people you really want to please are the ones you aren't making time for.

Who cares if your local Realtor association gives you an award at Realtor prom as your fellow agents cheer if your kids at home are starting to forget the sound of your voice?

Who cares if you outsell everyone in your office if your spouse is left sitting at home wishing you would give even a quarter of the effort to your marriage as you do to your clients?

Who cares if you're the mom who volunteers for everything and is known as the "go-to person" when your own family can't even rely on you?

Who cares if you gain the whole world but lose every important relationship in your life?

Success is just window dressing. Love is the real prize.

For example, say you committed to being on the local PTA, which meets twice a month. If the PTA is legitimately and appropriately in your hierarchy, keep it. But for our purposes, let's say it does not make the cut. Here's what you might say to the PTA leader:

> I'm sorry, but I need to step down from the PTA committee. I've realized that my attention is not going where it needs to go, so the reason I am stepping down is to give more time and energy to (insert the higher-priority item, such as "my family"). I know this decision might (insert any difficult circumstances that might arise, such as "it may be harder on you and the other committee members"), and for that I really am sorry. I said

yes to this when I should have said no, and though I really do not want to let you down, I absolutely cannot let my family down.

The PTA committee can find another member. Your kids can't find another mom or dad.

It might take a few days of courage to work through these challenging conversations, but they will be worth it. I've been the chairman of a local pregnancy center nonprofit for the past six years, and I've absolutely loved it. It makes me sad to think my time there is coming to an end, but it is. Why? Because that time and energy needs to be redirected to my hierarchy of family and wife.

So build your hierarchy, start unwinding from commitments, and then get in the habit of asking yourself weekly, *On a scale of one to ten (ten being perfect and one being utterly lousy), how am I doing?* Ask that for each of your lines on the hierarchy. Whatever the answer is, ask the follow-up question, *What can I do this week to take it up a point or two on the scale?*

For example, say I'm at a six out of ten with Rachel. I then ask, *What can I do this week to make it a seven?* Maybe it's scheduling a date night, making dinner for her one night, or scheduling time for her out of the house while I watch the kids. Whatever it is, ask the questions and keep your attention where you want it to be.

You can do this.

Do less and do it better.

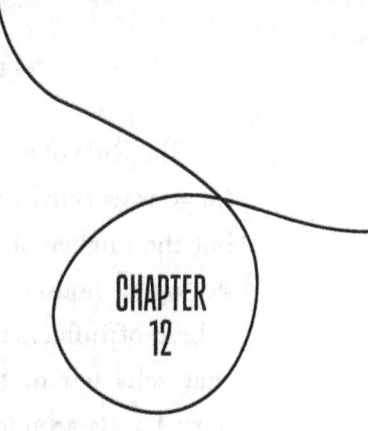

CHAPTER 12

Rule of 8s

Raise your hand if you use more than one source of lead generation. Go ahead, raise your hand. I know you're by yourself in that coffee shop drinking that latte and not wanting to look weird, but come on now, raise that hand. Now, keep your hand up if you have three or more sources. Four or more sources? Five or more sources? Okay, put your hand down.

For anyone who utilizes more than one way to generate leads, which is 99 percent of agents (I just happen to be the oddball of the group), here's the way to organize those sources. I call it the Rule of 8s. I learned a version of this concept from Russ Morgan and Joey Mure with Wealth Without Wall Street (to learn more go to wealthwithoutwallstreet.com) and adapted it to apply to salespeople.

The Rule of 8s is like the hierarchy of attention but for your working life. Most agents have an "everything but the kitchen sink" lead generation approach. They do open houses, door-knocking, expireds/FSBOs, sphere of influence, social media, and so on . . . and that sells ten to twenty homes a year. When January 1 rolls around, they aren't feeling a big swell of excitement for what's possible in the new year; they're already exhausted from thinking about all the work they have to do in hopes of just duplicating the previous year's sales.

Be a business owner, not just an agent.

This is not how a business owner operates. Be a *business owner*, not just an agent. Business owners understand the levers that create actual returns in their work. That is, a business owner knows if they follow their own PDA Formula and, say, posts twice a day on Instagram, they will sell thirty homes every year (of course, I'm just making up numbers). A business owner knows the input that will create the output—think Profitable, which is the P in the PDA Formula.

The Rule of 8s comes in to help grant you the freedom to focus on one type of lead generation at a time until you become so excellent at it that it's on autopilot. You've likely heard the term "habit stacking" before, where you develop one good habit then layer another one on top, then another, and so on. This is habit stacking for lead generation.

Develop one excellent lead generation habit and get your proficiency up to an eight out of ten. Once you're performing consistently at that habit for a few months, then and only then move to the next lead generation habit and build that one to an eight out of ten. Then, do it again. You're stacking your lead generation efforts.

Here's how the Rule of 8s works:

First, write out all your lead generation sources.

Second, cross off all the ones that do not align with who you are.

Third, rank the remaining sources from most effective to least effective.

#2 Social Media   ~~Farming~~

#1 36 Touch   ~~Door-knocking~~

~~Zillow~~   #3 Open Houses

Now, you have your prioritized list of lead-gen sources to develop. The magic happens in the habit stacking. You will develop your top source until it's an eight out of ten. All your focus and attention goes there until it is running almost on autopilot. Then, and only then, move to the next source. Focus solely on that until it's an eight out of ten and running on autopilot. Then, move to the next one, and so on. One at a time. I am not suggesting you ignore the other sources of lead generation while you focus on your top source; I am suggesting you hone in on improving just one source at a time.

The Rule of 8s

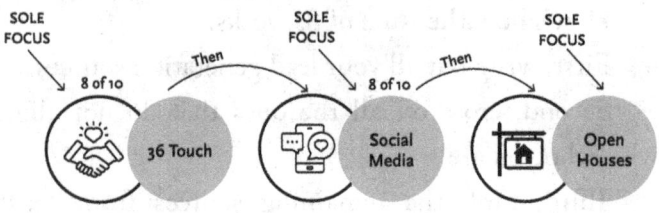

Here's what typically happens: We do not stay focused in one area long enough to ever develop it as a strength. We go to the gym, do one leg day (I hate leg day), then do an arm day, a back day, a shoulder day, a cardio day . . . and wonder why our legs aren't getting much stronger.

Have you ever seen a six-year-old turn sunshine into a laser beam? Of course you have; we all have. Maybe you even remember doing it yourself. All it takes is a magnifying glass. One small piece of glass can concentrate the power of the sun into a tiny focal point that will burn through a leaf or piece of paper. And guess what? That's all you need to spark a raging fire. And once it gets going, it can be darn near impossible to stop.

Focus long enough, and you can ignite something awesome.

That's the power of focus.

Focus long enough, and you can ignite something awesome. So, keep the magnifying glass on the first lead-gen source until it catches fire, then shift the magnifying glass over the second source and catch that on fire. Go one at a time until you have three different lead-gen sources all on fire, burning red hot, and producing qualified leads for you all at once!

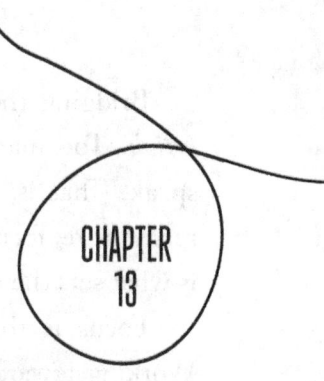

CHAPTER 13

The Right Next Thing

"You know the definition of hell on earth? It's when you're lying on your deathbed and the person you could have been meets the person you became."

Ouch. I heard someone say that a long time ago, and it's stuck with me. It's a new way to think about "the dash" that I mentioned all the way back at the start of this book. But here, maybe it's not a *dash* as much as it's a *gap*—a gap you have in your life right now, a gap between where you are and where you could be.

How do we bridge this gap? How do we get closer to our full potential? How do fish start swimming again and tree frogs start climbing trees again and bears start mauling people again? (Kidding! I'm just trying to squeeze as many animal references in as I can.)

Bridging the gap requires two things: *focus* and *action*. Too many agents only focus on focus, so to speak. That is, they get stuck getting ready to get ready. Sure, focus is great—essential, even. But action is what sets the top performers apart.

Focus is the easy part. (Well, the *easier* part.) Working toward that goal is where the rubber meets the road. That's when things get hard.

Working toward that goal is where the rubber meets the road. That's when things get hard.

One of the biggest struggles I have experienced in my own life and see repeated over and over in our world is a lack of focused direction. Where are we trying to go, and how are we going to get there? A pilot doesn't set out from Atlanta to Denver without a clearly charted course. The journey never goes exactly as planned; planes go off course constantly, but they always adjust and land where they intend to land. If the plane landed in Vegas instead of Denver just because the pilot felt like it, that pilot would be fired immediately.

Imagine if that pilot acted like we often do. They'd take off from Atlanta headed toward Denver, but thirty minutes in they'd hear how great it is in Dallas and shift direction. On the way to Dallas, they would hear that Salt Lake City is actually the place to be, and they would change direction again. On the way to Salt Lake, they would hear from their pilot friend who's having a blast in San Diego and would shift course again. That's literally how we run our businesses, and yet we are confused why it doesn't work.

If the pilot hits rough air, do they just turn around? If they run into turbulence, do they say "forget it" and just land wherever they feel like it? If the pilot is tired of flying do they just crash the plane into the ground? Of course not. We see the "buckle up" sign, and we gear up for whatever is coming. And guess what? The turbulence *always* ends, and we always end up in Denver where we intended to go in the first place.

Business and life are much like this. We start in one place with a goal to get to another, better place. But when we hit turbulence, instead of putting on our seat belts, we eject from the plane, or we land somewhere else and convince ourselves we are happy with the new destination. I've got to tell you, though, if the plane bound for Cancun for our first wedding anniversary had decided to land in Birmingham, Alabama, just because the pilot got tired of working hard, neither I nor Rachel would have been happy travelers.

I had a health coach once challenge me after I'd had a bad day of eating—which I call Mondays, Tuesdays, Wednesdays, Fridays . . . I had chowed down a really high-calorie, unhealthy breakfast this particular day. Since I'd already "ruined" the day, I figured, *What the heck? Why not eat whatever I want all day since I already blew it?*

Not the wisest approach, right?

I got on a call with my coach, and he said, "Garrett, one bad meal is one bad meal. That's okay. Just because you blow a tire on your car doesn't mean you total the vehicle."

He was right. Just because we have one bad "meal" in our business or life does not mean we should throw in the towel and go full-on in the wrong direction. Let me encourage you (as I often have to remind myself) to resist the urge to simply give up. On the other side of your internal struggle is the life you're looking for.

The big question is: *Where are you headed?*

Where are you headed in your marriage? In your family life? In your business? In your health journey? In your spiritual journey? In your friendships?

Your scoreboard gives you that destination—front and center. That's the easy part. The hard part is picking a path, sticking to it when the seat belt light turns on and the plane gets rocked a little, and continuing on until you land where you wanted to go.

With so much information flying around our industry these days, it's all too easy to get stuck in the muck of contradictory advice. We might read one book that argues for social media, and then the next book we read champions cold-calling. We listen to one podcast that explains how to grow our business by hiring agents, and the next podcast argues for virtual assistants. Then, we just sit there confused. The more competing opinions we have, the more our businesses look confused.

I'm all for getting different opinions and new ideas, but let's face it: As real estate agents, we're usually hopeful and optimistic, and we tend to think everything will work and will be amazing. So, we are easily swayed by our opinions and actions.

Confusion causes chaos. Clarity causes profits.

Rachel and I homeschool our kids. If one day we showed Haddie, our oldest, a way to do her math problems, and then we showed her a completely different way the very next day, that would be unproductive, unhelpful, and confusing. She needs us to give her a clear, consistent direction for her learning.

It's the same way in business and in life. We need a clear path, and we need to stick to it long enough to actually learn it and then go execute it before we start veering off in a different direction.

Confusion causes chaos. Clarity causes profits.

Failure to execute once we know the right path—and failure to make adjustments as needed along the way—can leave us stuck in a dead stop while everyone else's business seems to be zipping right by us.

In my second job out of college, I was assistant to the Christopher Newport University president, Paul Trible. He is a brilliant man, a former US senator, and a champion of his vision. It was an honor to work with him.

One of my main roles was driving him to various meetings and speaking engagements. One time, we were in northern Virginia, right outside Washington, DC. Imagine being in the middle of way too many cars driving way too fast. We were headed to a meeting during rush hour, so the chaos on the road was palpable. Somewhere in the back of my mind, I was always scared of crashing and being known as the guy who killed President Trible. Not the reputation I wanted.

We had the GPS on in the car, which put me in the far-left lane of the four lanes of traffic. All of a sudden, President Trible looked up and said, "No, no. This isn't right. Take this exit." He pointed all the way to the right, only about a quarter mile ahead.

The GPS disagreed and squawked, "Stay in the left lane for half a mile," while the president of the university was telling me to cross three lanes of traffic during rush hour at fifty miles an hour before I missed the exit that was about fifty feet in front of us.

Somehow, by the grace of God, I maneuvered to the far-right lane and onto the exit ramp with President Trible still fully intact. He turned toward me, put a hand on my shoulder, and said, "Well done, young man." And that was that.

We have one voice telling us to go left and another telling us to go right, and we get stuck. It's no wonder our business and our life aren't where we want them to be. We constantly allow voices to pull us back into the wrong lane, the lane of stagnancy. A much wiser approach is to pause, take some time to think, evaluate our options, pick a voice to listen to, get in the lane that will lead to our destination, and take purposeful action in the right direction. *That's* success. And if you don't know exactly what to do, then just do the right next thing.

Okay, Garrett, I get it, you might be thinking. *But I'm confused and stuck in the wrong lane. Now what?*

First of all, hear me when I say this—*so am I*. Whoa, shocker! An author admitting they don't have it all figured out? That's right. Just ask anyone who knows me. I'm on this journey too. It is so hard to keep going in one direction long enough to actually arrive at that destination. I have the fear of missing out just like you. I want to be involved in everything. I want to get to do all the things and go to all the events and sell one hundred homes a year while somehow also being fully present with my family and seeing my friends and going on vacations and never being stressed out.

But guess what? That kind of life does not exist. So what can you do?

You can strive for excellence in all that you do. Strive for bigger goals. Strive to be a better parent, spouse, and friend. Strive for all of those. And also . . . give yourself grace. You're only human. You can only do what you can do. That's why you have to choose which things to focus on and which things to let go of.

You *can* live an amazing life by doing less, not more. That's my challenge to you.

As you simmer in the confusion of, *What's next?*

As you sit in front of your scoreboard and wonder, *How am I going to accomplish this?*

As you question whether you really have what it takes.

All I want you to do is ask yourself one question: *What is the right next thing?* Answer that question, take the necessary action, and then stop and ask the same question again. The journey of a thousand miles begins with just one step.

The right next thing could be deciding on what kind of lead generation is most authentic to you. Or it could be working on your hierarchy of attention.

Or it could be creating a lead generation recipe. It might even be planning a date night with your spouse. Whatever it is, you get to choose. If I've learned anything in business, it's this: The more often I choose the direction I intend to go, the more often I arrive at my destination.

You can do this.

You can get there.

I'm rooting for you.

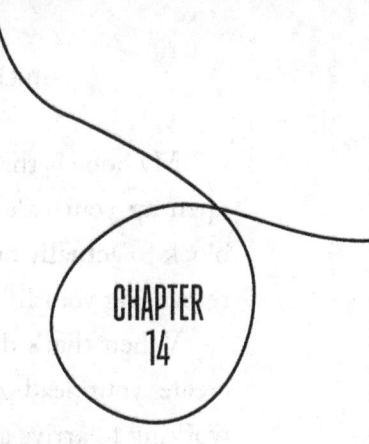

CHAPTER 14

Conclusion: So What?

This is the part of the book where I'd love to leave you with a mic drop moment—or whatever the literary equivalent of that would be. Maybe a book-slips-out-of-your-hands-while-your-jaw-hits-the-ground moment? Either way, the truth is, all I really want to leave you with is encouragement and a gentle pat on the back to spur you on in the right direction.

If you could choose to be anywhere in your life on a scale from one to ten—with your relationships, your business, your health, your finances, your spiritual walk, and so on—would you choose to be right where you are? Are you a 10 in every category? If not, then let's get to work. Remember, education is amazing, but you can never *think* your way into a new life; you can only *act* your way there.

My hope is that when you close this book you will open up your calendar and set aside just a two-hour block to actually build your scoreboard. That's Step 1, refocusing your life.

When that's done, schedule a two-hour block to create your lead-gen recipe. That's Step 2, actively working to arrive at your intended destination.

Then schedule one more two-hour block to create your hierarchy of attention. That's Step 3, being intentional with your attention.

Change comes from constantly, patiently, persistently choosing to head in a purposeful direction despite all the other pathways offered to you.

Remember, no permanent change comes from one moment of motivation or one burst of focus. Change comes from constantly, patiently, persistently choosing to head in a purposeful direction despite all the other pathways offered to you. Your scoreboard is your pathway.

One day, someone will be looking at your headstone, see some dates and a dash, and think, *I wonder what their life was like.*

What would you like the answer to be?

CONCLUSION: SO WHAT?

"He sold a ton of houses, made crazy amounts of money, won all the awards at Realtor prom, was on all the shows, blah, blah, blah . . ."?

Or do you hope they say, "She was an incredible wife, a devoted mother, excellent in all she did, and beloved by those she loved and who loved her"?

Which is the life you would choose?

Which is the life you *do* choose?

Remember way back in chapter 2 when I told the story of the woman who came up to me after I gave a talk on the scoreboard? She was a solo agent and mom who had sold fifty-five homes the previous year. Everyone was asking her what she was going to do in the coming year, so she told them she'd sell sixty or seventy homes because she thought that's what she was supposed to do.

She told me, "But after hearing your talk, I've decided I'm not going to aim for sixty or seventy sales; I'm going to intentionally sell *thirty* homes this year, and it's going to change my life!"

Well, that wasn't the whole story. Her full comment was, "Garrett, I got into this business to have more time freedom because I wanted to pick up my daughter from school every day. But guess what I've never done? I've been so busy selling houses that I can never get to the school on time. So, this year, I'm going to intentionally sell thirty homes just so I can do what I really want to do—pick up my daughter from school."

I wish you all the best in making the space to "pick up your daughter from school"—to put first things first, to set your priorities, to run your business rather than the other way around, and to experience the balanced breakthrough that leads into a more joyous, fulfilling life.

You've got this!

acknowledgments

This book represents many years of trying to figure it out—how to find success in business without missing the little years of my kids' lives. It is the culmination of hard work, continual learning, and incredible mentors who pointed me in the right direction time and time again.

First and foremost, Jesus. He is the way, the truth and the life. I can willingly let go of worldly pursuits and keep my feet firmly planted with my family because I know this life is just the beginning—it's not the true prize. The true prize is a personal relationship with Christ for eternity. Seek to know Him and find true "success".

To my wife: Without your belief in me, I never would have started in real estate. You've supported me, believed in me, encouraged me, and allowed me to fail. You've given us five incredible children and are raising them while supporting your crazy, entrepreneurial husband. I love you more than I ever thought possible.

To my kids: Only one of you can read as of this publishing but know that I wrote this for you. I refuse to miss your little years. I've pursued balance as vigorously as I could so I can show up for you as often as possible. I love you all more than you will ever fathom, and I want to set a good example to each of you. I hope you each grow up to love Jesus and stand on my shoulders to impact the world far greater than I could have imagined.

To my business partners through the years—Dave, Jesse, Keith, Tyler and so many others—you all changed my life. Thank you for your wisdom, your guidance, your work ethic, and your deep friendship. No one succeeds alone.

To my mom: I know you are gone now, but I want you to know how much you impacted my life. When you passed away, I began rethinking everything. I wondered and asked the Lord how I could make a meaningful impact on the world. I wanted to leave a legacy of service, just as you so masterfully exemplified. Thank you for being the best mom I could have imagined.

To my dad: I am honored to be your son. Thank you for the countless phone calls, the wisdom, and the encouragement throughout the years. You have been an invaluable part of my journey. Thank you for

CONCLUSION: SO WHAT?

setting an example as both a man and a father that I strive to emulate.

To my awesome publishing and launch team—Becky and Kia at Forefront Books, who graciously walked this newbie through all my thousands of questions; Brad Byrd my literary agent who was the first to believe in me and opened this door to my incredible team; Jenn DePaula who has been a master at helping me understand how to market this book; Allen Harris who helped make the book so much better through his editing; and so many others—thank you.

To everyone else who is not named but has been with me on this journey; thank you. Every person has played a role in shaping me—and therefore shaping this book. I couldn't have done it without you and cannot continue to do it without you. I hope we all take stock of what's truly important in our lives and start showing up better for those we love most.

endnotes

1. Linda Ellis, "The Dash," Best Poems Encyclopedia, accessed July 3, 2025, https://100.best-poems.net/dash.html.
2. Keith J. Cunningham, *The Road Less Stupid* (Keys to the Vault, 2017).
3. Gary Keller, *The Millionaire Real Estate Agent* (McGraw-Hill Education, 2004).
4. *The Simpsons*, season 12, episode 9, "HOMR," written by Al Jean, directed by Mike B. Anderson, aired January 7, 2001, on Fox.
5. "Where Basketball Was Invented: The History of Basketball," Springfield College, accessed July 3, 2025, https://springfield.edu/about/birthplace-of-basketball.
6. Nir Eyal, *Indistractable* (BenBella Books, 2019).
7. Melissa Dittmann Tracey, "Home Sales Weaken up against Rising Headwinds," National Association of REALTORS®, October 19, 2023, https://www.nar.realtor/magazine/real-estate-news/home-sales-weaken-up-against-rising-headwinds.

8. Jon Stubbs, "Average Real Estate Agent Commission Rates (2025 Survey)," Clever Real Estate, May 28, 2025, https://listwithclever.com/average-real-estate-commission-rate/#rates-by-state.
9. Robert T. Kiyosaki, *Rich Dad's Cashflow Quadrant* (Plata Publishing, 2011).
10. Kris Tibbetts, "4 Ways to Turn Past Real Estate Clients into Repeat Business," McKissok Learning, April 14, 2021, https://www.mckissock.com/blog/real-estate/4-ways-turn-past-real-estate-clients-repeat-business/.
11. Vivek H. Murthy, "Our Epidemic of Loneliness and Isolation: The U.S. Surgeon General's Advisory on the Healing Effects of Social Connection and Community," 2023, https://www.hhs.gov/sites/default/files/surgeon-general-social-connection-advisory.pdf.
12. Daniel A. Cox, "The State of American Friendship: Change, Challenges, and Loss," The Survey Center on American Life, March 10, 2025, https://www.americansurveycenter.org/research/the-state-of-american-friendship-change-challenges-and-loss/.